HARRY STYLES

HARRY STYLES

PHOTO-BIOGRAPHY

ELLE COWEN

Plexus, London

CONTENTS

Chapter One

TEENAGE KICKS

'A dream is only a dream . . . until you decide to make it real.'
– Harry Styles

Though Harry was born in Evesham, Worcestershire, on 1 February 1994, he was still little more than a babe in arms when the Styles family uprooted and relocated to leafy Holmes Chapel – a sleepy hamlet which lies tucked away from view within picturesque east Cheshire countryside some twenty miles south of Manchester.

With both his parents working – Des Styles was an operations manager for a leading finance corporation, while Anne worked part-time in an office – when Harry was two he began attending the Happy Days Club & Nursery School. Once Harry got over the initial shock of the nursery's unfamiliar surroundings, he enjoyed himself enormously – especially when he was allowed to doodle away with food colorants on slices of bread before toasting and eating his efforts.

In September 1998, Harry, or 'H' as he was known within the family, made the switch from nursery to school at the nearby Hermitage Primary. Despite having dutifully dropped him off at the nursery for the past two years, Anne admits to getting all teary-eyed at the thought of her little boy going off to 'proper' school. Harry, however, wriggled free of Anne's hand and bounded through into the Reception classroom in his immaculately-pressed uniform of grey trousers, white polo shirt and navy-blue pullover, without so much as a second glance over his shoulder. Anne wanted to let her little boy get on with it in his own way, yet at the same time couldn't quite bring herself to leave him in another's care. And despite having already gone through the emotional shredder with Harry's older sister Gemma, she nevertheless loitered outside the school for an hour or so in case she was needed.

'Happy days' is how Harry remembers his time at Hermitage Primary – as revealed in One Direction's very first book, *Dare To Dream*. But that doesn't mean to say he didn't suffer at the hands of classroom bullies on occasion. 'I think the most important thing is to make sure you tell somebody. Make sure you talk to your parents, or let somebody know,' he said in a recent interview with the ezine *KansasCity.com*. Thankfully, Harry wasted little time in enlisting the help of a trusted teacher. When asked if he had a message for those of his fans who were suffering similar torment at the hands of a school bully, Harry urged them to do as he did by speaking out rather than suffering in silence.

Having bested the bullies, Harry was finally free to be himself and, as he was already very close to Gemma, he thought nothing of playing with the girls in the class. 'I used to be friends with girls as well as boys,' he later reflected. 'I wasn't one of those boys who thought girls were smelly and didn't like them; I was kinda friends with everyone.' Harry's circle of friends was expanded further thanks to his pitching in with the school football team. 'When I started playing for the local team in goal I made friends from other schools as well, which meant I had a lot of mates. I've always liked being around people and getting to know new people, so I've always had a wide group of friends.'

Like most boys his age, Harry enjoyed watching football as much as he did playing it, and supported Manchester United. Less typically, he was an enthusiastic performer in school plays. 'I once played Buzz Lightyear in *Chitty Chitty Bang Bang*,' he revealed. 'I know that sounds a bit weird, but basically when the children hid from the Child-Catcher in the toy store they had Buzz and Woody in there, so I got to dress up as Buzz.' Another 'weird' role came when he played an Elvis Presley-esque pharaoh in the school's adaptation of *Joseph*

'I wasn't one of those boys who thought girls were smelly and didn't like them; I was kinda friends with everyone.'
– Harry Styles

And The Amazing Technicolor Dreamcoat. When he played Barney – a mouse who lives in a church – in the following year's play, Harry embarked on a Buzz Lightyear-esque raid of his elder sister Gemma's room, and 'borrowed' a pair of her school-uniform grey tights. 'I had to wear [the] tights and a headband with ears on and sing in front of everyone. I like to think I was a good mouse,' he subsequently reflected. And anyone caring to see just how good a mouse Harry was can judge for themselves by going onto YouTube and typing in 'Harry Styles before he was famous'.

Of course, it wasn't only play-acting that gave young Harry a theatrical thrill: 'The first time I sang properly was in a school production. The rush that I got was something I really enjoyed and wanted to do more of. I always used to love singing. The first song I knew all the words to was "Girl Of My Best Friend" by Elvis. My dad introduced me to his music, and when I got given a karaoke machine by my granddad, Brian, my cousin, and I recorded a load of Elvis tracks. I wish I still had them so I could have a listen.'

On the surface, Des and Anne were a devoted couple with two adorable children, but behind the scenes things weren't all that they seemed. For some time now Anne and Des' relationship had been getting steadily worse, and having decided to go their separate ways, they sat Harry and Gemma down and explained the situation as best they could. Harry was only seven at the time and, though initially devastated, he quickly came to accept the situation. 'I remember crying about it when my parents told me they were splitting up, but after that I was alright,' he says in *Dare To Dream*. 'I guess I didn't really get what was going on properly. I was just sad that my parents wouldn't be together anymore.'

'I just didn't leave, it was a decision we should split,' Des told the Scottish newspaper *The Daily Record* in the wake of One Direction's success. 'Of course, I missed him [Harry] and Gemma, as you would unless you were some kind of monster. It was tough. I used to feed him every night, change his nappy, put him to bed when he was a baby, and then I was no longer living with them. I'm not an estranged dad. It was a tough time to leave them, but these things happen.' Harry and Gemma finally moved away from Holmes Chapel two years later, when Anne took over as landlady of a pub over in Northwich, where they

'I've always liked being around people and getting to know new people, so I've always had a wide group of friends.'
– *Harry Styles*

'The first time I sang properly was in a school production. The rush that I got was something I really enjoyed and wanted to do more of. I always used to love singing.'

– Harry Styles

were to live for the next five years. While relocating to Northwich didn't prove as taxing or unnerving as the family's move from Evesham, Harry was once again being taken away from everything he knew.

Though Harry remained at Heritage Primary, he was still too young to keep out-of-school contact with his friends. And with Anne having her hands full trying to run a pub, Harry was often left to find ways to amuse himself. This was easier said than done as the pub was so remote, and for a time Harry feared his only friends would be the animals occupying the surrounding fields. The experience of being attacked by a neighbour's temperamental goat soon after moving made him wary of wandering off on his own. Thankfully, there was a boy called Reg who lived nearby and was a similar age; the two quickly became firm friends. At weekends and during the school holidays, Harry and Reg would jump on their bikes and go off adventuring together. One adventure Harry never tired of was cycling the two miles or so to the Great Budsworth Ice Cream Farm, as he later revealed: 'That first summer Reg and I used to go [to the farm] every day. We'd borrow £2 off our mums and cycle up there

'Harry was always up for fun, wacky things, having a laugh, and he never cared what people thought.'
– *Will Sweeny*

and get an ice cream. I can remember that so clearly.'

Harry developed such a passion for freshly-made ice cream – especially his favourite honeycomb flavour – that one of the first things he did on joining One Direction was introduce Louis, Liam, Zayn and Niall to the farm's iced delights.

It wasn't too long after the Styles trio returned to Holmes Chapel in 2006 – by which time Harry and Gemma were enrolled at Holmes Chapel Comprehensive – that Anne met Robin Twist, the man destined to become Harry and Gemma's stepdad. 'I really liked him [Robin] and I was always asking mum if he was coming over. But she wanted to make sure that Gemma and I were okay with him being around,' Harry later revealed. 'She worried a lot, so in the end I used to text him and tell him to come over. I was really pleased when Robin proposed to mum. He did it completely by surprise while they were watching *Coronation Street* on Christmas Eve. I was at Abi's house at the time and I remember getting a call from my mum and how happy I was when she told me they were going to be getting married.'

Harry has since described the aforementioned Abi as his 'first serious girlfriend', but the honour of being his 'first love' goes to Felicity Skinner, an extremely pretty and equally precocious blonde who dated Harry for about a year when they were both fifteen. 'He was a really good boyfriend, very romantic, and, yes, shy,' she told *The People*. 'He was good-looking and obviously I found him very attractive. We were together for just under a year. It was a long-distance relationship, but it was a lot of fun. We just clicked straight away and got on really well. He was really sweet. It was puppy love and we were definitely each other's first loves.'

Long-distance love is difficult to sustain at any age, so a parting of ways was perhaps inevitable, as Felicity explained: 'There was no real reason why we split up. We just drifted apart. I don't think the distance helped, and we were really young.' Though their relationship was over, Felicity said she and Harry still kept in regular contact by phone and email, so she was aware of his escapades with White Eskimo, as well as his auditioning on *The X Factor*. Indeed, it was only when Harry suddenly found himself otherwise occupied as one fifth of One Direction that the phones calls ceased.

It was shortly after his split from Felicity that Harry took his first steps on the path that would lead to him joining One Direction. His best friend Will Sweeny had been playing drums for several years and regularly got together with another friend called Haydn Morris, who was learning to play the guitar. Will was desperate to get Harry involved and suggested he get hold of a bass guitar – despite the fact that he'd never played the instrument before.

Befriending Will also gave Harry his first taste of rubbing shoulders with a celebrity, as Will's mum was Yvette Fielding, the one-time *Blue Peter* presenter. Indeed, prior to Harry soaring to worldwide acclaim via *The X Factor*, having Yvette Fielding on its voting register was Holmes Chapel's sole claim to fame. In an interview with *Woman* magazine in March 2013, Yvette said she'd first encountered 'cheeky chappy' Harry when Will brought him home to tea one day shortly after the two began secondary school. 'The first time I met Harry, he did a sweeping bow and got down on his knees on the road. I thought, "What a joker, we'll get on well." When he came for tea he loved pizza and chips, and always put on these stupid voices. He called me his second mum; he and Will lived in each other's pockets, dressing and talking the same.'

Aside from copying each other's dress sense, mannerisms, and hair styles, the dynamic duo quickly realised they had a similar sense of mischief. 'We'd act like complete idiots in public. Harry would go into Tesco and pretend he had tourette's and walk around screaming and shouting,' Will revealed in an interview with *The Sun*. 'We'd throw things at each other;

'I knew I could hold a note, but I had no idea how I'd be.'
– Harry Styles

we'd create chaos and a bit of a mess. We played this game where you pick something up and throw it over your head without knowing where the other person is and they've got to try and catch it – Harry dropped stuff everywhere.

'[We] got told off in Waitrose once because we were screaming "Bogies!" as loud as we could. We would each scream, "Bogies!" louder than the other person; we would shriek until we were blue in the face. Harry loved it. He was always up for fun, wacky things, having a laugh, and he never cared what people thought.'

Will and Haydn had been getting together several times a week, but had inevitably tired of the limitations their two-man band imposed. 'We just played cover songs,' Will revealed. 'Then we said we should get a singer and a bass in, let's see how that goes. We had no intention of taking the band anywhere, we just wanted to see how it all sounded.

'Anyway, I said to Harry that I think he should learn the bass guitar, and he was like, "Yeah, I will, I like the bass,"' Will continued. 'So we went on the internet and we were looking at bass guitars [but] then we realised our other friend Nick [Clough] plays the bass. It was stupid making Harry learn the bass when Nick already played, so we asked him, "Why don't you sing?" He was like, "Oh, no, no, no, I don't wanna sing, I can't sing," and we were like, "Well, we think you should sing." You could tell he had a good voice. It needed work, but so does everyone's. But you could tell he could sing. He progressed really, really well. He was quite reluctant at first because he was self conscious about how his voice sounded. Every time he listened back to himself he'd be like, "Oh, it sounds awful!"'

Following her split from Harry's dad, Anne went that extra mile in encouraging her children to realise their ambitions. Yet, while no one could ever consider Harry a shrinking violet, singing in front of your mates takes incredible courage – regardless of your talent. 'I knew I could hold a note, but I had no idea how I'd be,' Harry later confessed. 'I'd always imagined what it would be like to be in a band, so I started practicing with them.'

As Will says, he and Haydn just wanted to jam with a full band and hadn't really thought about taking things to the next level. However, fate was to lend a hand when, within days of their coming together, their new music teacher announced that he was staging an in-house 'Battle of the Bands'. 'We were all ready to go and we started filling out the application form, but we didn't have a name and we couldn't think of anything,' Harry reflected. 'It got to the day before the show and we had to put something down, so we decided just to go for something completely random. I suggested "White Eskimo", and we hadn't thought of anything better, so we wrote that down and from then on that's who we were.'

> 'Harry confessed that he wanted to be a singer, but thought he couldn't make it. I told him to follow his dream.'
> – Yvette Fielding

'We had a week to practice [yet still] won the whole thing,' Will told *Sugarscape.com*. 'There were like twelve bands in there and we won the whole thing. We did a speeded-up version of "Summer Of 69" by Bryan Adams, and "Are You Gonna Be My Girl" by Jet. We won £100 between us, and like four CDs of our tracks being recorded which was absolutely terrible because it was done at the school.'

In *Dare To Dream*, Harry describes another White Eskimo live outing: 'A girl at my school said that her mum was getting married and wanted us to play at the wedding, so we rehearsed solidly for two days. We had a set-list of about 25 songs that the bride had chosen, and we learnt the lot. We got paid £160, which worked out at £40 each. And we got free sandwiches – what more could you ask for?'

According to Will's mum, Yvette, it was she who convinced Harry not to give up on his own rock'n'roll aspirations: 'Harry confessed that he wanted to be a singer, but thought he couldn't make it,' she told *Woman* magazine. 'I told him to follow his dream.' Harry, of course, followed his dream all the way to the pot of gold at the end of *The X Factor* rainbow, and according to Will, he did so with his best friend riding shotgun. One of Will's duties came in smuggling Harry in and out of his parents' home in Holmes Chapel without alerting the ever-present posse of teenage girls at the front gate. However, while Harry was doing his utmost to keep in regular contact with his best mate, as Yvette knew from her own experience in the spotlight back in the late-Eighties, his horizons had been irrevocably altered and, with the ever-increasing demands on his time, it was inevitable something had to give. 'Will [had] texted Harry to see if he was coming home,' Yvette revealed. 'They'd arranged to meet up but Harry never showed. There were tears from Will and he said, "I've lost my brother; it's like he's dead." Will was devastated, but had to learn to let go, because Harry was just gone. Harry broke Will's heart.' She then went on to add that she was 'gobsmacked' at how understanding Will had been. 'A lot of lads would be bitter, but he just says, "I hope somebody is looking out for Harry," and I think that's the mark of a true friend.'

'I didn't know if I had what it took to go on *The X Factor*, and I was really nervous about actually taking the step and applying.'
– Harry Styles

The X Factor was a firm Saturday-night favourite in the Styles/Twist household, and each week Harry would pass judgement on each act's merits. He also visualised himself walking out on stage to face the judges. Though he went so far as to send off for an application form, he couldn't quite bring himself to fill it in and post it. 'I didn't know if I had what it took, and I was really nervous about actually taking the step and applying,' he later confided in *Dare To Dream*. 'In the end, my mum filled out the application form and sent it off for me. I'm so grateful that she did. I often have those moments when I think, "What if she hadn't done that," or "What if so and so hadn't happened?" [She] came up to me a few weeks later and was like, "You've got an *X Factor* audition on Sunday," and I was like, "What?"'

Harry has never mentioned which song he chose for the initial non-televised auditions, but for his televised baptism by fire he opted for Stevie Wonder's Motown classic 'Isn't She Lovely'. Singled out by Dermot O'Leary for an impromptu Q&A session, it quickly became apparent that Harry was a natural in front of the camera; with his perfectly coiffed locks, cardigan, and scarf, he had a composure beyond his years. Ever one to call it as he sees it, Harry wasn't going to lie about life back in Holmes Chapel – not even on national television. 'It's quite boring,' he deadpanned to the camera, before conceding it was also 'picturesque'.

Despite the support of his family, who'd accompanied him to the studio, Harry was taking nothing for granted on audition day. 'Singing is what I want to do,' he told the camera. 'And if the people who can make that happen don't think I should be doing that it will be a major setback to my plans.' With a kiss of encouragement from Anne, Harry strolled out onto the stage as though he was at a school assembly. His calm demeanour wouldn't have gone unnoticed by Simon Cowell. Nor, of course, did the rippling wave of hormone-charged excitement which greeted Harry saying his name, or the collective 'ahhh' when he gave his age. Despite his obvious pluck, Harry's nerves got the better of him on a couple of occasions during the performance. From the audience's reaction it was easy to see they weren't going to hold the odd flat note against him, but Louis Walsh expressed concerns

as to whether he was ready to progress further. Thankfully, however, Simon and guest judge, Nicole Scherzinger – who who was standing in for Dannii Minogue while she was away on maternity leave – begged to differ. The former Pussycat Doll was left positively purring over Harry's performance and went so far as to tell him that she thought his voice was 'lovely'.

Harry's nervousness hadn't gone unnoticed by his sister Gemma, who was watching on from the wings: 'I couldn't believe how brave he was when his turn to go on stage came – it's my idea of hell,' she told *Mizz* magazine. 'His hands were visibly shaking, and backstage we all held our breath as he got a no from Louis. But, of course, Simon and Nicole said, "Yes." For the next few weeks, he only let mum and me listen to him as he practiced in the bathroom.'

Having made it through to the third and final day of *The X Factor*'s Bootcamp phase, Harry chose to perform a slow-rocking ballad originally sung by Oasis's Liam Gallagher, and it seemed like the perfect opportunity for him to shine. However, as was the case with his future bandmate Liam, his version of 'Stop Crying Your Heart Out' failed to grab the judges and both Simon and Nicole began to question whether Louis hadn't been right all along. When speaking to *The Independent* newspaper following One Direction's debut album entering the US chart at Number One, Simon reflected on Harry's *X Factor* auditions: 'At the time there were a couple of people, Harry and Liam, who were really good on their first auditions and we were really disappointed that, for whatever reason, they didn't make the cut on the second round.'

Needless to say, Harry was crushed on being given the verdict. But while Simon and Nicole were 'disappointed' that Harry hadn't lived up to his initial promise, they weren't quite yet ready to say goodbye, and Nicole put forward the idea of strengthening the Groups category by selecting five boys and four girls from the rejects and having them pool their talents. 'I practically put One Direction together with my hands tied behind my back,' she later joked to *fanpop.com*.

Harry has since admitted to being a bit slow on the uptake when asked to remain behind for some mysterious interview. 'Looking back, it's surprising that we didn't click on a bit quicker. We were all kind of like sat looking like [thinking] "five teenage boys that they've kept back . . ." The best moment for me out of the whole thing was when we were told we were going to be put in a band together. I'd spoken to Louis, Zayn and Niall at Bootcamp and I remember thinking, "This is going to be a lot of fun."'

Modest as ever, Simon – who would be serving as mentor for the eight acts in the Groups category – has since insisted that he was responsible for putting the boys together. 'I met

'Harry came up with the name One Direction – because we were all going in the same direction as a group.'

– *Zayn Malik*

them as solo artists to begin with,' he told *Rolling Stone* magazine in April 2012. 'Each of them individually had very good auditions. We had high hopes for two or three of them in particular, and then it all kind of fell apart at one of the latter stages. Interestingly, when they left, I had a bad feeling that maybe we shouldn't have lost them and maybe there was something else we should do with them. And this is when the idea came about that we should see if they could work as a group. We invited these five guys back – they were the only five we cared about.'

Rather than mentor their respective charges within the cramped confines of the television studios, each judge whisked their eight acts off to rather more secluded surroundings. With Simon overseeing the Groups, One Direction and similarly-assembled girl group Belle Amie would be flying out to southern Spain and taking up residence at the music mogul's palatial retreat alongside Diva Fever, Hustle, Princes and Rogues, The Reason, Twem, and F.Y.D.

However, before heading out to the airport and their date with destiny, Harry and his new-

found band of brothers underwent a seven-day team-bonding session in his own neck of the woods – though probably not far away enough from his mum's prying eyes for his liking. With Holmes Chapel being relatively close to Manchester airport, it served as the perfect location for the boys to set up camp – especially as the camp came in the form of Harry's mum and step-dad's guest bungalow. Though there was just one bedroom, the luxury bungalow had been recently refurbished, and came with state-of-the-art mod cons and a fully-fitted kitchen. Oh, and that's not forgetting the heated swimming pool. 'It was a new experience for all of us because it was like living in a student flat,' Harry reflected. 'My mum and Robin completely left us to our own devices. We all put in some money and my mum put a load of food in the fridge and we were left to get on with it. I cooked dinner for us one night [but] other than that I think we ate Super Noodles most days. We'd do ten minutes of singing practice, then play football for three hours, have a swim, [and then] drive to KFC. We were just messing around, but it was a really good way of getting to know each other's personalities.'

Aside from having a week to get to know one another's strengths and weaknesses, the boys were also expected to think of an imaginative name for the band. And guess who delivered the goods? 'Harry came up with the name One Direction – because we were all going in the same direction as a group,' Zayn revealed. 'Funnily enough, it was the first name we came up with, and we were like, "Brilliant, we'll go with that one."'

Harry and the other boys also thought it 'brilliant' to have Simon as their mentor. 'It was amazing when Simon walked out and we knew we'd got him,' Harry later revealed. 'We all went mad, and the next moment we were all laughing our heads off when he said, "You had that dreaded thought it could have been Louis, right?" We would have been happy with any of the four judges looking after us, but I think secretly everyone wants Simon to be their mentor.'

Despite the pressure he must have been feeling being so far from home, Harry was happy to let the chips fall where they may. 'Spain was so weird because we were still getting to know each other and then all of a sudden we were getting on a plane together for what felt like a holiday,' he later reflected. 'I think we suddenly felt really grown up because we were in this big competition and, even though the *X Factor* staff were there, we were looking after ourselves to a certain extent.'

'We would have been happy with any of the four judges looking after us, but I think secretly everyone wants Simon to be their mentor.'
– *Harry Styles*

And for all those wondering how Simon viewed the boys' shenanigans while they were in his care: 'If people are badly behaved sometimes – so what? I'm fine with that; at least they're having fun. You have to have some sort of control, but at the end of the day you want to have the personalities through so it is fun. They are entering the music business for all the right reasons – and that is not to sit in the library till three in the morning.'

For their make-or-break five minutes in the spotlight the boys chose to perform LA alternative rock outfit Ednaswap's 1995 hit 'Torn', which, though a beautiful soft-rock ballad, went largely unnoticed until covered by Natalie Imbruglia two years later. Simon thought their performance was a 'little bit timid', as they chose to take turns at singing the verses rather than reworking the song to show what they could do as a group. However, he obviously saw enough in those five minutes to justify his – or Nicole Scherzinger's, depending who you choose to believe – decision to bring the boys together and put them through as a group. 'They're cool; they're relevant,' he deadpanned. 'This is going to be a hard decision.'

> 'I wanted to tell the world, I was so happy.'
> – Harry Styles

The only 'hard decision' Simon had to make at that point in time, however, was whether to bother waiting until after *The X Factor* final – which he was already convinced One Direction were going to win hands down – to sign the boys up to his label Syco and whisk them off to

the recording studio. While he was careful to keep his poker-face from slipping in front of the camera, his mind was already aimed in One Direction, as he subsequently explained to *Rolling Stone*: 'When they came to my house in Spain and performed, after about a millionth of a second. I tried to keep a straight face for a bit of drama for the show . . . The second they left, I jumped out of my chair and said, "These guys are incredible!" They just had it. They had this confidence. They were fun. They worked out the arrangements themselves. They were like a gang of friends, and kind of fearless as well. The more I got to know them, the more I liked them and the more I trusted them. They had good taste and they understood the kind of group they wanted to be. They didn't want to be moulded. I [wasn't] interested in working with people like that, either.'

Having learned how to wring every drop of tension from a televised situation, when the time came to announce his supposedly difficult decision, Simon purposely kept the boys wriggling on the hook until all five were fit to burst. 'My head is saying it's a risk, and my heart is saying you deserve a shot,' he said. 'And that's why it's been difficult, so I've made a decision. Guys . . . I've gone with my heart – you're through.'

Harry was over the moon and wanted to shout it from the highest mountain, but he and the others were under strict instructions to keep their success to themselves – for the time being, at least. 'We had to keep it quiet from everyone else, which made it a bit weird,' he later revealed. 'I wanted to tell the world, I was so happy.'

Chapter Two

FACTOR 'X'

'It's a weird and wonderful feeling to have
your home town all rooting for you.'
– Harry Styles

After a few days of relative normality back home, Harry once again packed his travel bag and boarded a train bound for London, where he reconvened with his bandmates and set up home at the *X Factor* house with the show's fourteen other finalists. Of these, several already stood out as potential winners – including Dannii Minogue's 27-year-old singer-songwriter, Matt Cardle.

For One Direction and the rest of the hyper teens, living away from home with people who were relative strangers must have been pretty daunting. And though Harry and the boys had lived away from home before – for a week of unsupervised mischief in Holmes Chapel – nothing could have prepared them for the intensity of the *X Factor* house. With their popularity increasing by the day, simply popping out for some fresh air created a host of logistical problems, as Liam explained in an interview with his local newspaper, *The Wolverhampton Express & Star*: 'It's weird when we go out and get chased by paparazzi. There will be about eight photographers there just taking photos of you walking down the street. It's very weird. It's hard to get used to, but it's cool.'

Having had the family's guest bungalow as their personal playpen, Harry in particular was bemused by the postage stamp-sized room (the smallest in the house) where he and the others could – if everything went to plan – end up spending the next ten weeks. And with boys being boys, cleanliness and household chores were never going to be their top priorities. 'We had a lot of luggage and there was too much stuff in the room, so it ended up being a bit grim,' Harry later said of the experience. 'We did try to keep [things] tidy, but the longer we were in the show the more stuff we accumulated, and the room seemed to get smaller and smaller.'

These close confines, however, didn't deter Harry from shedding his clothes when the mood took him. 'Stripping off is very liberating. I feel free,' he said. 'It's always a spur of the moment thing, but no one seemed to mind. I think Mary [Byrne] secretly liked it . . .'

Many, if not all, of Harry's rapidly-expanding fan club would have given anything to have been in Mary's shoes that day. And had it not been for the spoilsport censors, they still might have caught a glimpse of Harry in the buff – and his extra nipples. 'One time I had to do a naked video clip for ITV2 [*The Xtra Factor*] where I was standing there with no clothes on and the boys had to pass various objects across me, keeping certain parts covered,' Harry

revealed. 'That was the plan, but at one point Zayn didn't move the book he was holding quickly enough and the cameraman got a bit of an eyeful.'

With Harry now footloose and fancy free, following his recent split from Felicity, the gossip columns were soon hinting of a romance between him and Cher Lloyd. Though the two were often snapped having a laugh together, their relationship was never anything more than platonic.

When the seventh *X Factor* series finally got underway for real, even the cynics who were questioning One Direction's right to be in the finals had to admit that the boys brought a brand-new dynamic to the competition. In keeping with the theme of the opening heat – Number One Singles – Harry and the boys came bounding onto the stage and launched into Coldplay's 'Viva La Vida'. By the song's end, it wasn't only the studio audience and viewing public who were swept away by their youthful exuberance – even the industry's movers and shakers sat up and took notice.

'You are, in my opinion, the most exciting pop band in the country.'
– *Simon Cowell*

In hindsight, it's easy to see that Simon's choice of song for the boys that night was a subliminal statement of intent: not so much 'Viva La Vida' (which translates as 'long live life'), but rather 'long live One Direction'. Affirmation that he was holding a potentially winning hand came the following week with the audience's reaction to their rendition of Kelly Clarkson's 'My Life Would Suck Without You'. 'You are, in my opinion, the most exciting pop band in the country. There is something absolutely right,' he brazenly declared, as though daring Dannii, Cheryl or Louis to challenge him.

As for Louis, his mind was on the singers rather than the song, and he declared that every

'Stripping off is very liberating. I feel free.'
– *Harry Styles*

'Every week we're all in total disbelief that we've got through and you can see it on our faces.'

– Harry Styles

schoolgirl up and down the country was going to 'fall in love with One Direction'. But by this point in the competition, Louis' prediction was already a reality, as Simon confirmed in an interview with *Rolling Stone*: 'Once they were on the show, it was unusual because in an instant, we had hundreds of fans outside the studio [and] that doesn't happen very often.'

For week three – Guilty Pleasures Week – the boys performed Pink's piano-led blues ballad 'Nobody Knows', an apparently autobiographical tale of her battle against depression. However, by the time they'd finished the song, the studio was a sea of happy faces, with Cheryl Cole going so far as to declare on air that One Direction were her own 'guilty pleasure'.

It would seem that the public at large were of a similar opinion, and with further faultless performances of Bonnie Tyler's 'Total Eclipse Of The Heart', and Kim Wilde's 'Kids In America' on weeks four and five respectively, Harry and the boys suddenly found themselves being pursued by a crowd of swooning females wherever they went, from the London Dungeon to the Pride of Britain Awards, and the *Harry Potter And The Deathly Hallows Part 1* premiere. In a little over a month, One Direction had gone from being an ad hoc combo making up the *X Factor* numbers to the hottest new boy band in the country.

Each week, special guests including Katy Perry, Bon Jovi, Rihanna, and Kylie Minogue were brought in to add a little magic to the proceedings. Week six saw a boy-band bonanza, with JLS, Westlife, and Take That – who were giving their first public performance since Robbie Williams' prodigal return – all performing in the studio. Having so much testosterone under one roof was perhaps asking for trouble – more trouble than the in-house security could deal with. Things got so hand of hand that the show's anxious producers were forced to call on the assistance of riot police to cope with the horde of over-excited girls running amok in the surrounding streets and bringing traffic to a complete standstill. While no one was pointing any accusatory fingers in his direction, Harry certainly didn't help the situation by tweeting: 'Can't wait to meet JLS, Westlife and Take That . . . Everyone should come down on Sunday.'

> 'It's brilliant to be home because this time next week we could potentially have won the show.'
> – Harry Styles

What no one knew until later was that Harry came within a whisker of missing the show entirely owing to a mystery ailment. 'At soundcheck we'd only just begun singing and, when it came to the bit where I sang, I started feeling really ill. I felt like if I'd sung I would have been sick. I didn't understand it; I'd never had stage fright that had actually prevented me from performing before. It was really strange.'

Regardless of whether it was something he ate before leaving for the studio, or his nerves simply getting the better of him, it was inevitable that the strain of being the most talked-about boy in the most talked-about band in the country, if not the world, was going to take its toll on Harry's mind and body at some point.

Though they lived with the fear of elimination, life at the *X Factor* house was one long party for the contestants. If anyone was feeling down, Harry and the boys could usually be counted on to lighten the mood by playing pranks on one another. However, not everyone

was a fan of Harry's high jinx. According to *The Daily Mirror*'s studio insider, while the contestants had been in the studio recording the Help for Heroes charity single someone thought it would be amusing to have Harry 'jokingly rugby tackle Wagner as he walked out of shot'. However, it seems no one bothered to let Wagner – who had vacated the *X Factor* house after just two days because of the noise – in on the joke. 'The next thing he knew, Harry was play fighting him to the ground and Wagner didn't realise the camera was still rolling. Incensed, he shook Harry off and squared up to him, locking foreheads. It was all pretty hostile and the atmosphere afterwards was terrible.'

The atmosphere didn't remain terrible for long, however, as Wagner finally received his marching orders the following Sunday. Aside from waving goodbye to the belligerent Brazilian, that week also saw One Direction perform 'Summer of 69' in the studio. One can only imagine what was running through Harry's mind while he was on stage singing the song that had spelled victory for White Eskimo back in Holmes Chapel to millions of people – including Will Sweeny, Haydn Morris and Nick Clough.

Two days after One Direction had claimed their place in *The X Factor* Final alongside long-standing fellow favourites Matt Cardle, Rebecca Ferguson, and Cher Lloyd, the boys went on a whistle-stop promotional tour of their respective home towns to meet and greet the people who had helped them achieve their dream. Harry admitted to being blown away

'When us five stood behind the doors for the first time on the live show, for that first song. For me that was the best moment.'
– Harry Styles

by the reception which greeted their arrival in Holmes Chapel: 'It's brilliant to be home because this time next week we could potentially have won the show. Every week we're all in total disbelief that we've got through and you can see it on our faces. We didn't expect to get through the judges house stage, never mind to the final. We're absolutely loving it.' When asked for his reaction to seeing the entire village festooned with banners, balloons, bunting and signs saying 'Welcome Home Harry', he added, 'Everyone's been brilliant. It's a weird and wonderful feeling to have your home town all rooting for you.'

While gearing up for *The X Factor* Final, One Direction frantically rehearsed Elton John's 'Your Song' and Robbie Williams' 'She's The One'. However, with rumours about Simon's intention to sign Cher Lloyd to his Syco label regardless of what happened in front of the camera running rife, the question on everyone's mind was had One Direction's fate already been sealed? In fact, they needn't have worried. When quizzed as to his intentions, Simon let it be known that Cher wasn't the only finalist he had his eye on. Indeed, it seemed that all four finalists could expect a one-on-one meeting immediately after the final – no matter which of them came out on top in the voting. Where the boys were concerned, Simon's advisor Sinitta said: 'Simon definitely wants to manage them. He knows they've got massive potential.'

As for Louis Walsh, he'd worked with enough boy bands in his time to recognise the value of One Direction. 'Of course, we need another boy band,' he told reporters. 'There's always room for boy bands, and they are the perfect boy band. There's a whole new generation that are going to love One Direction. They're a young Westlife or Take That.'

Just as they had on the opening Saturday of the ten-week live-show countdown, and again on week seven for a performance of the 'Heroes' charity single, for part one of the 2010 final, all sixteen acts came together for one last communal *X Factor* jamboree. The song

they performed was Irene Cara's 'Flashdance .
. . What A Feeling' – and what an adrenaline
rush each and every one of them must have
experienced as they walked out onto the stage.

With the bookies' firm favourite Matt Cardle
getting the business end of things underway
with a flawless rendition of Dido's 'Here With
Me', and with Rebecca Ferguson also putting
in a note-perfect performance of Corrine Bailey
Rae's 'Like A Star', Harry and the boys took to
the stage knowing the slightest error could prove
fatal. And with an estimated fourteen million
tuning in at home, could anyone have pointed
a finger if nerves had finally gotten the better of
them? However, the boys nailed it. Indeed, one
could say they made Elton's Top Ten hit 'their
song' on this particular evening.

The guest performers of the night were
Rihanna and Christina Aguilera, both of
whom also performed duets of their songs
'Unfaithful' and 'Beautiful' with Matt and
Rebecca respectively. With One Direction set
to perform Robbie Williams' 'She's The One',
the anticipation in the studio was palpable, and
when the boys came on with the man himself, the
sudden upsurge in decibels threatened to raise
the roof. Once the high-pitched frenzy – which
took even Robbie by surprise – had subsided,
Louis declared that he'd 'never seen a band
cause so much hysteria so early in their career'.
Dannii echoed his sentiments and applauded the
hard work they'd put in to reach the final: 'You
were thrown together, you deserve to be here,
and I'd love to see you in the final tomorrow.'

Cheryl was equally rapturous in her appraisal,
saying she'd enjoyed watching the boys grow
with each passing week, and that she felt they
deserved to be in the final. Simon was the last
to pass comment and, having taken time out
to acknowledge that Matt and Rebecca had
delivered note-perfect performances, he went on
to praise his charges for having given '1,000 per
cent', before telling them that it had been 'an
absolute pleasure' working with them: 'I really
hope people bother to pick up the phone, put
you through to tomorrow because you deserve
to be there.'

While it's doubtful the boys got much sleep the night before, come Sunday showtime they all appeared as bright-eyed and bushy-tailed as they had on week one. Following Matt Cardle's spellbinding rendition of Katy Perry's 'Firework', One Direction surprisingly sang 'Torn' – the very same song they'd performed at Simon's house in Spain. True, it was a far more professional and polished effort second time around, but why Simon opted for a song the audience was already familiar with instead of allowing the boys to show their versatility at the most vital stage of the competition only he knows.

Famous for his clashes with Simon, Louis' response was a surprise to everyone. Full of praise for the boys' flawless harmonies, the oft-fiery judge hadn't a bad word to say about One Direction's déjà-vu moment. Dannii and Cheryl were equally enthusiastic, and told the boys that they had a great future ahead of them. Simon, still convinced he was holding five aces in his hand, said that he would love to hear One Direction's name read out at the end of the show because, in his opinion, they deserved it. In the end, of course, this wasn't to be with host Dermot reading out Matt and Rebecca's names instead.

'As soon as Dermot reads out Rebecca's name you can see all our faces drop, and our fans in the audience kind of slumped,' Liam later reflected. 'It wasn't that we believed the hype when people said we were going to win, but we couldn't help but hope.'

When *Digital Spy* asked Harry what had been his outstanding *X Factor* highlight, he didn't even hesitate and told the website: 'When we walked in and saw the studio for the first time. Then, when us five stood behind the doors for the first time on the live show, for that first song – for me that was the best moment. That was where we were actually doing it, the real thing, for the first time. That was a big moment.'

Even the most jaundiced One Directioner had to concede Matt was a worthy winner.

But as Louis predicted immediately after the show, One Direction had all the necessary ingredients to make them the new Beatles, Take That, or Westlife. And while Louis would have willingly given his right arm to sign the boys to his stable, Simon had no intention of sharing One Direction with anyone else. The boys could also count on an enthusiastic Robbie Williams to fight their corner should the need ever arise. He was so impressed with how far they'd come in so short a time that he jokingly announced he was 'having twelve months with Take That, and then three years with One Direction'.

Nonetheless, in typical Simon fashion, Mr Cowell kept the boys waiting before giving them the good news that Sony [Syco's parent company] would be bidding to sign them up in the morning. 'I tried to stay as calm as possible, but on the inside I was terrified,' Harry later revealed. 'As soon as Simon told us we had a record deal and I started crying again and I sat there thinking, "Why am I crying? If this works out it's going to totally change my life." My life had already changed so much, but this was the moment that told me I didn't have to go back to doing what I did before – at least not for a while.

'I couldn't wait to tell my family the news, but of course we had to keep it quiet. I went back downstairs to the bar area because there was a little party going on, and I think my parents could tell from the look on my face what had happened.'

The boys were obviously given strict instruction to keep the news of the Sony proposal under their hats while an official brief was prepared, but by the following morning, the internet was buzzing with news of One Direction's £2 million record deal. While *The X Factor* Final was being dissected in playgrounds everywhere, the boys busied themselves with packing up their belongings and relocating to the nearby W Hotel, where the *X Factor* wrap party was set to be held that same evening. Even though Christmas – and Louis'

> 'As soon as Simon told us we had a record deal and I started crying again and I sat there thinking, "Why am I crying? If this works out it's going to totally change my life."'
> – Harry Styles

nineteenth birthday – was just around the corner, there was no immediate let up in sight for the boys: their days filled with management meetings, and their evenings taken up with guest appearances at various clubs in and around London. 'The reception we got in the clubs was amazing because we were out there doing proper shows with a set-list of songs,' Liam enthused. 'We could have carried on doing that for weeks but then Christmas rolled around, and I think we were all in need of a bit of a break after the madness of recent months.'

While he found himself missing the day-to-day camaraderie he and the other boys had built up in the five months they'd been together, Harry took advantage of the festive break to kick back with the family, as well as catch up with his mates. 'Loads of my friends wanted to catch up, so things were quite busy,' he later revealed. 'But I didn't want people to think that I'd changed and I didn't have time for them or whatever.'

The majority of his friends were naturally over the moon at Harry's success, but as Louis, Liam, Niall and Zayn were all finding out, some people he'd thought of as friends were showing their true colours. 'Some people have made comments and distanced themselves from me without actually letting me know,' he said. 'When you've been close to someone it's hard when they start acting that way towards you. I'm not going to chase after people and beg them to be my friend, but I wouldn't want them to think I don't care, because I do.'

Chapter Three

C'MON, C'MON

'Work hard. Play hard. Be kind.'
– *Harry Styles*

No sooner had the fairy lights been stored away for another year, than Harry and the boys were whisked back to Syco HQ in London, where – in close consultation with Simon – they began planning a strategy for the coming year. They already knew they'd be accompanying Matt, Rebecca, Cher and six other *X Factor* live show finalists on a nationwide tour, and the precious few days until then were taken up with meeting and greeting various producers, engineers, and songwriters – all of whom would be crucial in developing the boys' song ideas into a debut album. Meanwhile, their evening schedule was rapidly filling up with an ever-growing number of promo appearances. Despite the heavy workload, to the delight of their fans, the boys also found time to put pen to paper detailing their lives to date for a book called *One Direction: Forever Young: Our Official X Factor Story*. Devoted Directioners duly rushed to pick up a copy – or five – of this glossy tome, sending it straight to the top of *The Sunday Times* bestseller list within one week of release.

As with any public appearance by the delectable authors, book signings brought shopping centres to a near-standstill. Harry would later confess to finding signing his name awkward as he hadn't thought to practice beforehand, but he enjoyed himself all the same: 'We were excited about [the book] being out there and hoped that some fans would buy it, but we didn't realise just how many would get it. The fans that came along to the book signings were incredible. I got given lots of turtles because I once said I liked them – it's so cool when people remember little things you've said.'

January also brought their first taste of life as a signed Syco act – in the form of an all-expenses-paid trip to Los Angeles. 'LA is something else,' Harry enthused upon his return. 'Everyone you see looks like they're famous. We did some recording in this really cool complex where there were loads of different things going on. In one studio they were recording the backing vocals for *Glee*, and then Randy Jackson's office was 100 metres away, so we went to meet him.'

Aside from meetings with über-producers Nadir Khayat (aka RedOne) and Carl Falk, the boys were given ample free time to see the sights and to shop hard. 'I literally raided Abercrombie & Fitch,' Harry chuckled. 'Louis reckons I bought every single T-shirt they had in there. He's exaggerating, but I did get quite a few.'

Further evidence that One Direction were fast becoming a pop phenomenon came on their return to the UK, when – with a hullabaloo not seen since the Beatles were at the height of their fame in the mid-Sixties – thousands of screaming girls descended *en masse* on Heathrow airport to welcome the boys home. 'We were told that there were about two hundred people waiting for us, so we were ready to sign autographs and things,' Zayn explained. 'But when we walked out this whole swarm of people came towards us, so we had to run back inside the airport. There was no plan, so we just held on to each other and ran.'

If *The X Factor* served as the pad from which One Direction's career was launched, then the ensuing X Factor Live Tour was the rocket which propelled them into the stratosphere. Following intense rehearsals with a live band in London, the boys then travelled up to Wakefield and set up home at Light Structures, where they perfected their dance routines; infusing each one with just the right amount of swagger. Having grown accustomed to performing in front of a full house, the band found it strange to repeatedly run through their live set without an audience. '[It's] hard when you're in an empty warehouse performing to no one,' Harry explained. 'We had to practice putting talking bits in between songs, which also felt weird because we'd be talking to an audience of six crew members, and even they didn't respond.'

Having to run through their five-song routine – 'Only Girl', 'Chasing Cars', 'Kids In America', 'My Life Would Suck Without You', and 'Forever Young' – over and over again must have been challenging. But Harry, at least, is a believer in the old adage that practice makes perfect: 'Putting everything we'd learnt into practice was the ultimate pay-off for all the hard work we'd done,' he beamed. 'I can't even begin to describe what it was like when we all stood on stage together for the first night of the tour in Birmingham. I think that first arena performance was different to anything else we'd ever done in terms of how much energy we put into it, and how much we moved around the stage.

'It felt almost natural being [up] there, even though it was also completely and utterly surreal. There were times when we all looked at each other, and I could tell we were all thinking the same thing – "This is incredible!" The rush you get being on stage in front of so many people is indescribable. I wish everyone could have that feeling. I can be so tired and feeling like I'm in a bad mood, then I get on stage and I feel amazing. There's no feeling like it.'

The X Factor 2011 Tour, which had been extended to a staggering 51 dates due to frenzied demand for tickets – or, more pertinently, demand to see One Direction in the flesh – got underway with four sell-out shows at the 16,000-capacity Birmingham LG Arena over the weekend of February 19/20. Unsurprisingly, Matt and Rebecca – the only other two acts allowed a five-song set – were given a rousing welcome by the sell-out crowd, but they, along with Cher, Aiden Grimshaw, Katie Waissel and the others, were merely serving as warm-up acts for the main event – regardless of where the boys appeared in the running order.

All five boys were buzzing at the reception they'd received from the fans. 'The first night was phenomenal and took us completely by surprise,' Liam later enthused. 'Nothing could have prepared us for what we faced that first night. When you look out into the audience and someone's got your name on a banner, it doesn't really sink in that it's yours.'

'The rush you get being on stage in front of so many people is indescribable. I wish everyone could have that feeling.'
– *Harry Styles*

The tour's final show came at the Cardiff International Arena on 9 April. All the performers there had first got to know each other while living at the *X Factor* house, and after seven weeks spent travelling the country together, that evening's aftershow gathering was tinged with sadness, as everyone knew this was the last time they would all be in the same room together. Despite the gruelling schedule, Harry was enjoying himself no end: 'I loved the tour so much I never wanted it to stop. I didn't even get homesick because we were so busy we didn't get time to think about it, but I actually felt really guilty about that.'

Not that it played too much on his mind. No sooner was the tour over than he and Louis were jetting off on a ski trip to Courchevel, France. This wouldn't be the only occasion when Harry and Louis would be requiring their passports. The time had come for the boys to get busy laying down tracks for their hotly-anticipated debut. In this process, Stockholm, Sweden, was to be their first port of call, where tracks were laid down at both Cosmos and Kinglet Studios. Next on the agenda was the boys' second visit to Los Angeles, where, aside from more time in the studio, the boys would also be filming the promotional video for their debut single, 'What Makes You Beautiful'.

While en route to the City of Angels, Harry let his halo slip by engaging in some mile-high jinx – stripping off for the bemused female flight attendants operating in the first-class cabin. Then, during a day off from recording, he got naked again to go skinny-dipping in the Pacific surf. Later he was up to his usual tricks horsing around at the funfair on Santa Monica Pier with several of the girls from the promo video (shot in neighbouring Malibu). One girl in particular, Madison, caught his eye.

> 'I loved the tour so much I never wanted it to stop. I didn't even get homesick because we were so busy we didn't get time to think about it.'
>
> – *Harry Styles*

'Harry and Madison were inseparable,' an insider enthused to *The Sun*. 'They really hit it off and all the other boys kept teasing them both. They exchanged numbers and arranged to meet up when Harry was next in LA.'

To the American girls, Harry, with his cheeky smile and bouffant bounce, was the fourth Jonas Brother, but unlike the purity-promoting trio, Harry was single and ready to mingle with whomever he chose. 'I'm a seventeen-year-old boy, so I like girls, but I prefer having a girlfriend,' he declared to *We Love Pop* magazine upon his return to the UK. 'I like having someone I can spoil; somebody to call up in the middle of the night and just talk to. I like getting close to someone like that.'

Needless to say, Harry's newfound fame meant there was no shortage of girls desperate to be the one he might call up in the middle of the night when he was feeling a bit lonely. As per usual, the media was equally desperate to keep tabs on Harry's love life, and each day brought fresh rumours of his latest love interest. During a promotional tour of Ireland, following the advance release of the promo video to 'What Makes You Beautiful', Harry decided to play the media at its own game. When asked by *The Sun*'s dogged reporter what made a girl beautiful in his eyes, he replied 'I like cute girls who are funny,' before adding that he didn't 'really have a type'. The reporter was still feverishly scribbling away when Harry paused for thought: 'I do like girls with short hair,' he said at length. 'But I also like girls with long hair . . .'

'What Makes You Beautiful' shot straight to the top of the UK Singles chart and sold close to 154,000 copies in its first week of release in September 2011. Sony revealed that the single had smashed the label's existing pre-order record, and soon the song became the highest-charting debut for a UK act on the US Hot 100 since Take That back in 1998, entering the

'I like having someone I can spoil . . . somebody to call
up in the middle of the night and just talk to.
I like getting close to someone like that.'

– Harry Styles

Billboard chart at Number 28. It would eventually reach Number Four, selling over three million copies in the process.

'What Makes You Beautiful' was co-written by Rami Yacoub, Carl Falk and the boys' old *X Factor* pal Savan Kotecha. But while Simon wasn't yet ready to trust them with writing their own material, he allowed the boys an equal say in the choice of song for the all-important debut single. 'When we were recording in the studio we knew instantly that we wanted this track to be our first single. I think for us, we wanted to release something that wasn't cheesy, but fun,' Harry told *MTV News* shortly after the single's stateside release. 'It kind of represented us . . . I think we found the right song.'

As well as performing several times during *The X Factor*'s 2011 live shows, One Direction also made a couple of notable guest appearances on the series' ITV2 spin-off *The Xtra Factor*, co-hosted by one Caroline Flack – a name destined to become notorious among 1D's fans. After the band appeared on *The X Factor* 'Guilty Pleasures' live show, Harry posted the following comments on the show's official website: 'Obviously, we like a girl to be attractive but it's all about the banter – standard! And I like a babe with a talent – you need to be good at something. Like tennis! Now, that's cool. If Caroline Flack is reading this, say "Hi" from me. She is gorgeous.'

Though he'd made no secret of his intentions towards Ms Flack, what the outside world wouldn't discover until a year after the event was that Harry had enjoyed a three-month fling with Heart London DJ, Lucy Horobin, who, fifteen years his senior, was the same age as Caroline. Harry had first encountered the elfin, freckle-faced Lucy back in August at the Manchester-based station Key 103, where she was working when the boys dropped in to promote 'What Makes You Beautiful'. While Lucy was playing the single, Harry jumped to his feet and mimed along to the lyrics, playfully clasping his hands to his heart and mouthing the words, 'I love you.'

Harry and Lucy stayed in touch via Twitter and Facebook, but their online chatter had escalated to open flirting by the time the boys returned to the station the following month. Eventually, Lucy – who'd been married to her husband Oliver for just over a year – was photographed leaving a plush Manchester hotel after a rendezvous with Harry. Once news of theaffair broke, Lucy found herself under cyber-attack from Harry's irate younger admirers, and was forced to take to Twitter to defend herself: 'To clarify, I haven't said ANYTHING to any press, nor do I wish to. Thank you to those of you who have said kind words today. Xxx'.

Harry appeared totally unrepentant when pressed for a comment about their affair by *The Daily Mail*. So much so, in fact, that when the paper enquired if he had an age limit where potential girlfriends were concerned, he nonchalantly replied: 'Anything up to my mum's age. She's 44!'

Meanwhile, the opportunity with Caroline that Harry had been waiting for finally presented itself towards the end of October, at an *X Factor* aftershow party at the W Hotel in London. True to form, super-confident Harry made a beeline for Caroline, and it isn't hard to imagine the other partygoers' surprise when Harry moved in for a kiss. What was even more startling was when Harry and Caroline left the party together, sharing the same cab home. None of the other revellers thought this worthy of comment – at least not to the media. Harry, however, couldn't resist dropping a hint into cyberspace: 'Sometimes things happen and you suddenly get a whole new outlook on life,' he tweeted.

Harry's fanatical female followers on Twitter were the first to realise something was afoot when reading Harry's, 'Woke up with man flu and a sore throat today,' in response to Caroline's earlier tweet: 'Woke up with the sorest throat and huge glands!!!'

The backstage area of any successful TV show is no different than the average school playground when it comes to spreading gossip, and it wasn't long before rumours of a blossoming romance were doing the *X Factor* rounds. In public, Harry initially kept up the pretence by saying while he 'would love to take Caroline out', he didn't want to 'share her with Olly'. But while Caroline might have been reticent to go public about their romance, Harry was smitten and didn't care who saw them together.

Chapter Four

HIGHS AND LOWS

'The reason why the fans are so dedicated is because I think they feel like they can really relate to us; like we're the kind of boys that you go to school with – and we are.'
– Harry Styles

By mid-November, all eyes should have been on the new crop of *X Factor* finalists. Yet, thanks to One Direction's sparkling debut record, there was only room for one act in the UK's music press. *Up All Night* slammed onto the chart at Number Two as the fastest-selling debut album of the year – and was only denied the coveted top spot by Rihanna's *Talk That Talk*. As with 'What Makes You Beautiful', the album – featuring thirteen tracks penned by Kelly Clarkson and McFly frontman Tom Fletcher, amongst others – proved a resounding commercial and critical success, topping the charts in Australia, New Zealand, Canada, and several other countries before the year was out.

The cynics who claimed One Direction were little more than manufactured puppets who'd contributed only three songs to *Up All Night* would be interested to learn that 1D were anything but a band of 'yes' men. In the words of Mr Styles himself: 'Some of the lyrics were about forty-year-old men pouring their hearts out. I can't imagine ever being quite that old,' he told *The Daily Mirror*. 'We said "no" to at least one song, but he [Simon] would much prefer us to be honest. Despite what people think, he doesn't want to be surrounded by lots of "yes" men. We get quite a lot of freedom and a say in what we do. Once we found our sound, we told Simon we wanted to keep it really young. Simon wants us to put a stamp on our music, so he appreciates our input.'

With the UK and the rest of the world's record-buying territories falling like dominos, there was only one direction left for the boys to go – and and that was stateside. November saw the boys sign a lucrative deal with Sony-owned US label Columbia Records. Columbia's co-chairman, Steve Barnett, told reporters that signing the boys was something of a no-brainer: 'Other artists in that category had gotten a little older. I just thought there was a void, and maybe they [One Direction] could seize and hold it.'

To promote *Up All Night*, the boys set off on a headline UK tour, commencing in Watford on 18 December 2011 and ending with a final date at Belfast's Waterfront Hall on 26 January 2012. The excitement amongst 'Directioners' (as the fans had taken to calling themselves) had reached fever-pitch by the time the tickets went on sale. With the majority of the venues selling out within minutes, further dates were added and, when those tickets were snapped up in a similar fashion, extra matinee performances had to be slotted in at the existing venues

HARRY

'Some of the lyrics were about forty-year-old men pouring their hearts out. I can't imagine ever being quite that old.'
– Harry Styles

in order to cope with the demand.

A surprise on the tour came when the boys posted an invitation via Twitter, saying that any girl who wished to be serenaded onstage need only name her band member of choice online to be in with a chance of making this dream a reality. On the opening night of the tour, 20-year-old Hollie Gilbert was the envy of every other girl there as she made her way up onto the stage, where Harry was waiting. But Hollie had barely retaken her seat when Twitter trolls launched spiteful attacks and, with those same trolls targeting the two girls selected for onstage serenades at subsequent shows, the boys were sadly forced to abandon this idea.

Following matinee and evening shows at Manchester's O2 Apollo Theatre just before Christmas, the tour was put on hold until the new year so Harry and the boys could celebrate the holiday with their family and friends. In the year or so since they'd each first set out in search of *X Factor* fame and fortune, the boys had been forced to decamp to London. Zayn, Niall and Liam each had their own base of operations, but with Harry and Louis being brothers from another mother, it didn't come as too much of a surprise to anyone when they announced they'd be sharing.

Their luxury flat – set within twenty acres of mature parkland in Friern Barnet, north London – quickly became the boys' hideaway hangout, as well as party central. The party Louis and Harry threw on New Year's Eve was particularly rowdy and, if reports in the media are to be believed, saw the boys 'stock up on beer, thirty bottles of vodka, a few crates of wine, and plenty of mixers'. Unsurprisingly, the majority of the attendees were female. And perhaps even less surprisingly, Harry was snapped with his arm around a stunning mystery blonde.

With work commitments keeping them apart, it seemed Harry and Caroline were managing to keep their romance low-profile, but that all changed shortly into the new year, when the pair were finally papped emerging hand-in-hand from the chic West End night spot Asia de Cuba. Needless to say, once the story went viral the media declared open season on Celeb World's latest couple. By this time, Harry had become accustomed to having his every move mapped

out in newspapers and magazines, but Caroline found the scrutiny unnerving to say the least. 'When you go to a public event you know there are going to be photographers there; it's their job,' she told *The Sun*. 'But it's weird when they are outside your house and when they turn up at your mum's house, and when you are driving down your street and you have to swerve because there are three cars behind you and three motorbikes following you wherever you go.'

It wasn't only the paparazzi that Caroline had to worry about now that her romance with Harry was in the public domain. Within hours of the story breaking she found herself under cyber attack from green-eyed Directioners – some of whom took their envy to extremes. The online abuse got so intrusive that Caroline felt compelled to respond: 'I'm close friends with Harry,' she tweeted. 'He's one of the nicest people I know. I don't deserve death threats.'

What no one knew until later was that Harry was receiving threats of a different kind from Simon Cowell, who feared that his relationship with Caroline might damage One Direction's clean-cut image. Indeed, such was his obsession with maintaining a wholesome profile that he forbade the boys to remove their tops during photo-shoots.

With his management having taken its rigid stance, Harry was forced to face up to the inevitable. However, unlike scores of other celebrity couples, he and Caroline parted as

friends. So when ugly rumours to the contrary began to surface, Harry felt honour-bound to tweet the truth: 'Please know I didn't "dump" Caroline. This was a mutual decision. She is one of the kindest, sweetest people I know. Please respect that.'

As for Caroline herself, she didn't have a bad word to say about her former flame in an interview with *The Sun*: 'Harry is adorable, he is a nice person. He was nice to me – we were nice to each other. He's brilliant, he is so much fun. First and foremost we are friends. We got very close for a time but that's between me and Harry . . . then we decided it was best to just be friends.'

Whatever the opinions of his fans, Harry's mum clearly bears Ms Flack no ill will. 'I have met Caroline, but I don't want to go into things about the two of them,' she told *Heat* magazine. 'That's over now. I never really thought about the age gap, but I had a [ten-year] age gap with Harry's dad, so I suppose that's what he saw. I don't think it's very important, to be honest.'

On Tuesday, 3 January 2012, the Up All Night Tour resumed with a show at the 6,500-capacity Windsor Hall, housed within the Bournemouth International Centre. As the clock crept ever closer to showtime, the tension inside the arena became physical in its intensity. So much so, that a mere ripple in the curtain or the lighting being adjusted brought shrieks of excitement.

Though the boys have always shared vocal duties, the shrieks were a tad more frenzied whenever it was Harry's turn to take centre stage, as *The Independent On Sunday* observed. Having commented on the 'ear-splitting screams' which greeted Harry's every word, the paper reported: 'mop-topped Harry is by far the most popular. Close your eyes and guess when Harry's on lead, from the spike in decibels. You'll never be wrong.'

The tour – inclusive of matinee shows at many of the venues – had seen the boys play to a collective audience of 500,000. With untold numbers of fans overseas equally anxious to see their heroes in the flesh, it was decided to extend the tour to take in Australia, New Zealand, and North America. As with the UK, tickets were snapped up as soon as they went on sale. The New Zealand-based news agency *Stuff.co.nz* reported that the 10,000 tickets for the shows in Auckland and Wellington had been snapped up in ten minutes, while the band's three Australian dates in Sydney, Melbourne, and Brisbane had sold out in just three minutes. A similar phenomenon was witnessed in the US, though this came as no surprise to Simon. In fact, the stateside trickle of interest in One Direction was rapidly becoming a downpour.

Syco's initial stateside strategy for *Up All Night* was to release the album on Friday, 23 March 2012, but owing to what Columbia Records described as an 'overwhelming fan demand' the album was rush-released ten days earlier. However, given Columbia's inspired approach to marketing – placing it within the fans' reach to bring One Direction to their hometowns via

'Please know I didn't "dump" Caroline.
This was a mutual decision. She is one of the kindest,
sweetest people I know. Please respect that.'
– *Harry Styles*

Facebook petitions and video comps – none of this should have come as a surprise. Columbia's promo campaign – launched around the same time as the album's UK release – proved an unqualified success. Not only did the band's Facebook following in the US soar from 40,000 to 400,000, but 'What Makes You Beautiful' sold in excess of 131,000 copies in the week following its release on 14 February – despite receiving no airplay whatsoever. Indeed, it wasn't until 28 February that Columbia finally issued the single to US contemporary hit radio play-lists. As a result of the enforced delay, radio programmers throughout America found themselves inundated with calls from irate fans demanding to hear the song. Johnny Wright, former manager of New Kids on the Block, Backstreet Boys and 'N Sync, told reporters: 'They are calling the radio station and the radio station is scratching its head, saying, "We don't even have that record yet." It's almost like the return of the Beatles. I call it hype, but it's positive hype, because it's all real. It's not manufactured. No one paid these kids.'

'We simply cannot believe that we are Number One in America,' an overwhelmed Harry told reporters on hearing the news that *Up All Night* had entered the *Billboard* chart at Number One. 'We want to thank each and every one of our fans in the US who bought our album and we would also like to thank the American public for being so supportive of us.'

While subsequently speaking about One Direction's unprecedented US success with *Rolling*

'We simply cannot believe that we are Number One in America.
We want to thank each and every one of our fans in the
US who bought our album.'

– Harry Styles

Stone, Simon offered his opinion as to why the majority of British bands had failed to crack America by saying it was simply due to most British acts trying to mimic their American counterparts and ending up with a sound 'somewhere between England and America, which means you fall smack down in the middle of the ocean [as] you don't appeal to either.' He was also more than willing to acknowledge the boys' own part in their rise to the top: 'Every record we made and we progressed with, it was always based off the feedback from the boys in the studio. If they liked something, we went ahead. If they didn't like it, we threw it in the bin. They were a big part of the selection process of the songs on the record.'

As the winner of Columbia Records' Facebook campaign hailed from Dallas, Texas, on 13 March, the boys conducted a meet and greet at the Barnes & Noble store at the Stonebriar Centre Mall in Frisco. But chaos ensued when an estimated 3,000 teenage girls descended on the mall, bringing it to a near-standstill. According to a local news report aired later that same evening, scores of fans were left battered and bruised following a frenzied stampede the moment the mall opened its doors.

While the boys (again on promo duty) were greeted by similarly hysterical crowds in

Massachusetts and Tennessee, the Annual Kids' Choice Awards – celebrating the very best in television, film and pop – passed without incident. The show was hosted by Will Smith and featured many famous faces. The guest of honour that evening was Michelle Obama and, proving anything but star-struck, cheeky Harry couldn't resist asking the First Lady if she and her husband had ever experienced any difficulty in having takeaway pizza delivered to the White House.

This, of course, was also the night that Harry first encountered his future flame Taylor Swift. According to *The Daily Mirror*'s secret source backstage, the 22-year-old beauty had confessed to having a crush on Harry. 'Taylor is a huge One Direction fan, and was excitedly bopping along to the boys when they performed on stage. Then she started chatting to Justin [Bieber] and told him how hot she found Harry.' The insider went on to reveal what happened when Taylor went backstage. '[She] was hanging around by the group's dressing room, and said a quick "Hello" to the guys. She started dramatically fanning herself afterwards, making out like she was overwhelmed, which got everybody laughing. She really likes Harry, but made Justin promise not to go on the record about it.'

While the boys were in LA during their January promo visit, *Heat* magazine conducted a poll of the world's '101 Hottest Hunks'. It didn't come as much of a surprise to find Harry, Louis, Liam, Zayn and Niall had all made the list – with Harry scoring highest of any of the boys at number eighteen. With the rest of the world finally beginning to acknowledge Harry's hotness, he was soon finding that simply striking up a conversation with a girl was enough to generate column inches of gossip.

Despite the hordes of teenage girls dreaming of life as Mrs Styles, Harry has always had an eye for the older woman. While seated on the next table to reality TV star Jillian Harris (an interior designer who shot to fame on *The Bachelorette* dating show) in the W Hotel dining room, Harry nonchalantly leaned closer to ask for her number. Jillian, however, was one 32-year-old who wasn't about to succumb to Harry's charms, as she later revealed to *The Sunday Mirror*: 'He [Harry] looked cute and adorable, but I could never date an eighteen-year-old. I don't think that's even legal in the US, is it?' Having explained that she'd required her more switched-on friend to tell her who One Direction were, she went on to reveal that Harry refused to take 'no' for an answer: 'We got up to leave [and] he walked straight up to me and said he would like to take me out for dinner. I didn't know what to say, I think I just laughed. Then he said he was playing a concert in Canada later this year. I told him that maybe my friend and I would come to the show. He said he would like that; then he asked for my phone number. I can't remember what I said. I don't think I was rude. I just told him I was way too old for him. He didn't seem too put out. He was very sure of himself actually.'

Chapter Five

IRRESISTIBLE

'I've always wanted to be one of those people that
didn't care that much about what people thought
of them . . . but I just don't think I am.'
– Harry Styles

Harry and the boys arrived in Sydney on Easter Monday, to commence the Oceanic leg of the 2012 Up All Night Tour. As with previous arrivals at Heathrow and LAX, the airport's concourse had been taken over by a throng of fans, who were all eager to snatch a fleeting glimpse of their heroes. Despite the luxuries afforded in business class, the long-haul flight still took its toll on the boys, and, having been shepherded from the plane and into blacked-out cars, they were whisked off to the five-star Sydney Continental Hotel. Some fans gave chase, and excitedly took their places among those 1D devotees who'd opted to set up vigil outside the hotel, their patience being rewarded when a topless Zayn appeared at the window. Another throng of eager Down Under Directioners had camped out overnight outside a pop-up shop that was stocking nothing but 1D merchandise – ranging from T-shirts, dolls, and hoodies to CDs and posters.

As this was their first visit to Australasia, the boys were given a couple of days off to acclimatise. They showed little sign of jetlag as they cruised around Sydney Harbour aboard a luxury yacht, soaking up the sun and goofing around like any other carefree teenagers. They'd long since become accustomed to having their every move monitored through the media's lens, and Harry, sporting a pair of brightly-coloured swimming shorts, casually stepped up to the rail and dived over the side, knowing images of his ripped torso would soon be splashed across the pages of dozens of newspapers around the world.

The fun and frolics extended into the evenings – especially for Harry and Zayn, who found themselves the centre of attention again after agreeing to serve as judges for a wet T-shirt competition in the Scary Canary bar. British backpacker Emma Carrigan was there to witness the boys' cheeky bar-side antics in person. 'It was crazy,' she told *The Mirror*. 'We go there every night and it has never been as mobbed as it was when the two of them walked in. The [girls] were bombarding the boys and throwing themselves at them. It was so bad that that one of their bouncers had to ask for an area to be cordoned off. When the wet T-shirt competition began, Zayn was just looking on and smiling, but Harry went crazy and kept shouting, "Come On. Come on!" They were just lovely guys having fun.' And who can blame them?

Harry and Zayn's mischievous nature was also in evidence during various promotional

'So we thought, what better way for us to meet people that we would get on with than by presenting the "Most Popular Female Talent" award?'
– *Harry Styles*

visits in the run-up to the gigs. Having both become enamoured with Nova FM's striking 20-year-old receptionist Anna Crotti, whom they'd met briefly before going on air, during the interview Harry said that Anna was 'lovely' and 'very polite', while Zayn commented on her 'beautiful eyes'. Zayn went so far as to obtain Anna's number and ask her out on a date. Anna had readily accepted, but was forced to cancel after coming under attack from jealous fans. The abuse wasn't only confined to cyberspace, however, as some girls took to calling the station and abusing Anna on the phone. She also had to deal with tearful mothers calling in, begging her to reveal details of the boys' agenda so their daughters could meet them. 'By the end of the day, it all got a bit too scary,' she told *The Mirror*. 'I didn't even want to walk home. It was so intense.'

Following another interview, Harry had one of the publicity team ring reporter Elle Halliwell and ask for her number, even though he couldn't have failed to spot her engagement ring! Elle, though 'flattered', respectfully declined.

Harry and the boys have always worked at least as hard as they play, and Friday, 13 April saw them perform two back-to-back shows at the 5,500-capacity Hordern Pavilion. British Directioners would have been puzzled as to why Harry and the boys were playing such relatively modest venues. The media were no doubt asking the same question, seeing as *Up All Night* had sold in excess of 300,000 copies in Australia and New Zealand. For once, it seemed Syco had miscalculated the boys' appeal, as they could have sold the tickets for the five shows several times over.

Niall won the heartfelt thanks of Harry's adoring fans by tweeting some saucy black and white pics of his pal stripped down to his Tommy Hilfiger boxers backstage. In one of the pics Harry appears to be shaving his legs, before playfully putting the razor to Liam's throat.

The Melbourne Herald Sun was enthusiastic when the boys performed at the city's Hisense Arena three days later, proclaiming them a 'cleverly cast pop band with plenty of personality unleashed at the perfect time and seizing their moment'. This was the night the boys were reacquainted with Dannii Minogue, who, despite her recent split from boyfriend Kris Smith, came along for the gig and a backstage catch-up.

While in Melbourne the boys performed 'What Makes You Beautiful and 'One Thing' at the prestigious Logie Awards, where they also presented actress Melissa Bergland with the

'I'm not really a pick-
up-line-guy – I don't
know what to do.'
– Harry Styles

Most Popular New Female Talent award for her role in *Winners & Losers*. While the boys were being interviewed on the red carpet outside the Crown Palladium, Niall said the only downside to their inaugural visit to Australia was they didn't 'really know anybody'. Before the interviewer could respond, Harry – looking very dapper in his dicky-bow and tuxedo – quipped: 'So we thought, what better way for us to meet people that we would get on with than by presenting the "Most Popular Female Talent" award?'

Next up was Brisbane, as covered by *Billboard* scribe Lars Brandle. 'Hysteria has followed them since they arrived in the country,' he wrote afterwards. 'And this concert served as a mass outpouring of delirium.' He too was struck by the passion of the 5,000 teen girls who turned out to see their idols that night, and 'created a noise so fierce, it would have drowned out most machines [of] the industrial age'.

During their stay in Queensland's state capital, the boys visited the Lone Pine Koala Sanctuary. Harry posted a picture of himself on Twitter with his newfound furry friend, Kat. However, Kat proved just as captivated with Harry as any of his two-legged admirers and – having pooed on him – stubbornly refused to relinquish her grip on Harry's T-shirt and had to be prised away by a member of staff.

There was no let up in the hysteria when the boys arrived in Auckland, where they were set to play two back-to-back shows at the Trusts Stadium. According to *stuff.co.nz*, hundreds of girls set up camp outside the boys' hotel (the luxury five-star Langham), while as many

'I know it sounds weird, and the rest of the lads tease me about it, but I just really enjoy cleaning – what can I say?'
– Harry Styles

more brought traffic to a standstill when the boys visited the 328-metre-high Auckland Sky Tower. While Louis and Liam literally jumped at the chance to throw themselves off the top of said tower (albeit safely attached to a bungee), Harry has no head for heights. Instead, he opted to keep his feet firmly on the ground – playing with Lux, their stylist Lou's baby daughter. Next on their meet-and-greet agenda was a visit to Eden Park to watch a Kiwis v Kangaroos rugby league match, where their arrival elicited as much interest as what was happening on the pitch.

Later that same evening, Harry was spotted in the company of another lovely lady, New York-born model Emma Ostilly, at the fashionable Grey Lynn's Gypsy Tea Rooms. They had met in New York the previous year when Emma appeared in the promo video for 'Gotta Be You', and Harry wasted little time in calling her after the boys arrived in Auckland. They were snapped while out and about in the city, and again kissing on the steps outside Emma's house in the early hours of the morning. According to *The Sunday Mirror*'s mystery insider source, Harry and Emma 'really seemed to have a connection and only had eyes for each other. They seemed very happy and relaxed and you could tell they have a history together.'

What the mystery source failed to mention was that Emma had a steady boyfriend called Sean Gallagher, who, needless to say, didn't take kindly to seeing pictures of his girl in the arms of another man. Fortunately for Harry, Sean, who was serving in the navy, was away on manoeuvres at the time.

On being asked if he and Emma were now an item, Harry retorted, 'No, she's just a friend.' When Liam cut in with, 'She's not his girlfriend either,' Harry added, 'No . . . she's working over here. I prefer not to talk about her.'

Within minutes of photos of the pair appearing online – one of which Harry had mischievously posted himself – the Twitter trolls were back and furiously venting. Harry was used to their cyber-sniping, but it was a whole new experience for Emma. And, with the abuse showing no sign of abating, she was forced to resort to closing her Twitter and Facebook accounts.

While Emma went into hiding, Harry and the boys flew on to Wellington, where they were due to give their farewell performance at the city's St. James Theatre. Before leaving for the gig, however, the boys were treated to an impromptu concert of sorts, when the 300 or so fans who'd set up camp outside their hotel (the Intercontinental) serenaded them for several hours.

Upon their return to the UK, the boys had a couple of weeks' downtime before heading over to Stockholm to begin work on songs for their follow-up album. As a reward for all the hard work they'd put in to date, Simon reportedly handed each of them a £2 million bonus. When pressed to confirm the rumour by a particularly pushy journo from *The Sun*, Niall joked: 'Simon Cowell is tight. That's why he's so successful. He's able to keep his money to himself – we're paid in jelly beans.'

Aside from splurging on designer clothes, Harry – having passed his driving test back in December – treated himself to a £100,000 black Audi R8 Coupé with grey side panels. (His car collection would soon be expanded to include a Porsche 911 Sport Classic, and Robin Twist's 4x4 Range Rover Sport). During the break, Harry drove up to Cheshire to show off his new car, and was snapped picking Gemma up from the train station and giving a lift to mate with a broken leg. It was in an interview with *OK!* magazine that Harry revealed that his passion for fast cars stemmed from a mate's dad being a classic car dealer. Most lads his age would have viewed the Audi or the Porsche as a 'babe magnet', but Harry, of course,

'Since we've been out here, it's been crazy. We're just riding the wave, working hard and having a lot of fun.'
– Harry Styles

didn't have to rely on flash accessories to score with the ladies and considered his top-of-the-range purchases as sound and sensible investments: 'If I didn't have fun with it [the car], I'd just end up a bitter old man,' he told the magazine. 'I think if you invest in the right things, cars can be safe as property.'

Back in London, Harry paid a visit to Liberty – Regent Street's most exclusive department store – to stock up on furniture and art fabrics for his new bachelor pad in east London, which had set him back a cool £575,000. Sharing with Louis had been tremendous fun, but his friend's relationship with long-term girlfriend Eleanor Calder was beginning to cramp his style. As Louis commented at the time, 'The worst thing about living with Harry is the constant stream of girls he is getting through our door – it's relentless!'

The two girls who remained constant fixtures in Harry's life, however, were his mum and sister. When speaking with *Mizz* magazine the previous year, Gemma revealed that she and her baby bro had grown closer despite Harry's 'hectic schedule and the occasional eight-hour time difference!' Since then, Harry's workload had doubled, but he still set aside time to Skype with Gemma, regardless of where he was in the world. Perhaps more than any of the One Direction boys, Harry remains especially close to his mother and whenever he is away he always takes the time to seek out little gifts for her; be it a pair of designer shoes, or a matching handbag, Harry never returns home empty-handed.

According to Yvette Fielding, Harry also splashed the cash on a luxury home for his mum: 'Anne's life has changed dramatically, it's like she's won the lottery,' she told *Woman* magazine. 'One minute she was worrying about a kitchen extension, the next minute her son bought her a gated mansion – the kind that only footballers can afford.'

Anne, or 'Foxy Coxy' as she is known to Harry's bandmates and male friends, is a natural when it comes to dealing with the media and happily agreed to grade her son's cooking and cleaning skills live on-air with Radio One DJ Huw Stephens. For all those wondering how Harry did, Anne gave her son an A- for his ability to cook a family meal, before revealing that his tidiness left plenty to be desired. So it would have come as something of a surprise to her – as it would to anyone who saw the state of the boys' room at the *X Factor* house – when Harry later bragged about his love of house-cleaning in an interview with *The Daily Star*. 'I've loved cleaning since I was little. I find it very relaxing and calming. I even watch all the TV shows about it to help me with ideas and stuff,' he told the paper. 'I know it sounds weird, and the rest of the lads tease me about it, but I just really enjoy cleaning – what can I say?'

> 'We're not really thinking too far ahead. It's all still sinking in, really.'
>
> – *Harry Styles*

Bizarrely, Anne has occasionally come under fire online; though what she could have done to upset the trolls is anyone's guess. Someone else who found herself caught in their spiteful sights was Harry's old school friend Ellis Calcutt – and all because she dared to accept his offer of a spin in his new Audi. Unlike Emma Ostilly, however, Ellis tackled the problem head on: 'Wow, you people are sooo quick to make up rumours!' she tweeted. 'Me & Harry went for a coffee together as we haven't seen each other since last year! We're only good friends and have been since High School. I have a lovely boyfriend called Phil, so you can stop spreading rumours about me and Harry dating each other because we absolutely are not!'

In any case, Ellis was way too young by Harry's standards. In an interview with *The Sun*, Harry reeled off the names of his dream women – Angelina Jolie, Kate Moss, and Kate Winslet – before attempting to hoodwink the paper, saying: 'I'm not really a pick-up-line-guy – I don't know what to do.' Pull the other one, Harry!

Someone Harry didn't need to bother practicing his pick-up patter for was 22-year-old actress Emily Atack, best-known for playing Charlotte Hinchcliffe in *The Inbetweeners*. Two years earlier, Emily had set her stall out by tweeting: 'Does Harry from One Direction HAVE to be sixteen?! Let's pretend he's eighteen at least! Then there would only be One Direction he would be going . . . to the bedroom!' Well, Harry was eighteen now, and only too happy to take Emily up on her offer. 'They're perfect for each other, they really are,' a friend of Harry's told *The Sunday Mirror* when news of their romance broke. 'They've been getting to know each other and keeping things quiet, but they're close. Harry has always had a crush on her and hoped he could get it together with her – and they eventually did.'

Harry's 'friends' were telling anyone willing to listen about him and Charlotte, but when *The Sun* asked him to comment Harry set the record straight, saying that while he and Charlotte had met up a couple of times, they did so as friends – they hadn't even kissed.

Having visited America as recently as March, Harry and the boys already had an inkling of what awaited them as they boarded a plane bound for Los Angeles. But no words of wisdom from Simon could ever have prepared the boys for the barrage of media attention

that was unfolding around them. On the same day the 22-date leg of the tour got underway with a show in Uncasville, Connecticut, *Dare to Dream: Life As One Direction*, went on sale throughout the US, and would soon top *The New York Times* Best Seller list. But the most telling indication of the boys' stateside popularity came with the *Up All Night: The Live Tour* DVD outselling the Number One album on the *Billboard* chart. The following month, Sony's CEO, Nick Gatfield, announced that he expected the boys to earn the label a staggering $100 million in the coming twelve-month period. 'What you might not know about One Direction,' he told reporters, 'is that they already represent a $50 million business and that's a figure we expect to double next year.'

The money was rolling in at Sony, but there were others within the industry beginning to question the logic behind Syco's decision to announce dates for a mammoth 100-date summer tour to promote the as-yet-unrecorded second album, while One Direction were still fulfilling obligations for the first album. 'It's insane,' *Rolling Stone*'s associate editor, Andy Greene, said via his magazine. 'They're working them like dogs, and printing money right now.'

The boys were having too much fun to question what was going on behind the scenes at Sony. 'Since we've been out here, it's been crazy,' Harry told reporters midway through the tour. 'It seems to have blown up a bit, it's been insane for us, we're just riding the wave, working hard and having a lot of fun. People are being so, so nice and [have] welcomed us so much, and for them to have taken the interest that they have in us feels pretty special.'

> 'At the moment, it appears I have,
> like 7,000 girlfriends. It's ridiculous.'
> – *Harry Styles*

And as for the future, he added: 'We're not really thinking too far ahead. It's all still sinking in, really. In Boston we did a meet-and-greet and these five girls came dressed as each of us. They do that a lot. It's cool.'

If bands were handed medals instead of BRIT awards, then One Direction would surely be in line for the gold. As the first British group to score an instant Number One on the American chart with their debut album, it seemed only fitting for Harry and the boys to be up on stage at the closing ceremony of the 2012 Olympics (held in London on 12 August). After Madness and the Pet Shop Boys had played, the boys rolled up atop a black-and-white patterned lorry to perform their teen anthem, 'What Makes You Beautiful'. Looking dapper as ever in a tailored suit, Harry was clearly enjoying his moment in the spotlight. 'For me the Olympics literally can't be topped,' he grinned in an interview with *Billboard* magazine months later. 'Just the feeling of being in that room, all our families were there . . . [it] was unbelievable.'

One month on, the boys were ready to release 'Live While We're Young' – the first single from *Take Me Home*, 1D's hugely-anticipated second album. Savvy Simon Cowell has been in the music industry long enough to realise that if something ain't broke you don't bother fixing it. So for the boys' sophomore offering, he called upon the same songwriting team behind *Up All Night*: Rami Yacoub, Carl Falk and Savan Kotecha. 'Swedes have been making great pop songs since Abba,' Falk told *The Independent* shortly after beginning work on the new album. 'We love melodies and nice chord changes.'

'We'll spend days, sometimes weeks, challenging the melody,' Kotecha added. 'The goal is to make it sound like anyone can do this, but it's actually very difficult.'

As promised, 'Live While We're Young' was another slice of pure bubblegum pop, and gave the boys a top-three hit on both sides of the Atlantic. *Digital Spy* awarded the single four out of five stars, saying 'it's little different from what we've heard before – but when you're the world's biggest boy band, it's no bad thing'. Hooked on the song's foot-tapping intro and feel-good chorus, *4Music* dubbed it 'insanely catchy' from the first listen.

Harry and the boys first performed their new single to a UK audience at the BBC Radio One Teen Awards on 7 October at Wembley Arena. Suspended high above the heads of their swooning fans, the boys serenaded hordes of screaming Directioners from a gravity-defying plinth. They also walked away with the three most coveted awards of the evening: Best British Single for 'One Thing', Best British Album for *Up All Night*, and Best British Act. Harry was bursting with joy at the hat-trick: 'Thank you again to BBC R1 for having us,' he tweeted. 'Thank you everyone who voted! So happy to win!'

Meanwhile, if the constant media speculation about his love life was to be believed, Harry seemed to have adopted 'live while I'm young' as his personal motto. And while most of these 'romances' turned out to be nothing more than tabloid gossip, one sultry beauty who did catch his eye was nineteen-year-old Cara Delevingne – aka the 'star face' of Burberry's 2012/2013 season and one of the hottest models of the moment.

The pair were first papped jumping into Harry's Range Rover Sport in the first week of

August (apparently their exit from the exclusive Olympic VIP Club at Omega House wasn't speedy enough). For once, though, the papers were behind with the story. An earlier – albeit unconfirmed – sighting of Harry and Cara apparently came when they were spotted lounging by the rooftop pool at Shoreditch House, another private members' club. They had, in fact, met earlier in the summer at the notoriously exclusive nightclub Le Baron in Mayfair, having been introduced by Harry's Radio One DJ pal Nick Grimshaw and Pixie Geldof.

Yet while Cara's older sister, Poppy, had already made it known to the world that she was crushing on Harry ('I want to 'sit on [his] lap,' she gushed in *Grazia*. 'He walked past me at the Aquascutum show recently and I was salivating. I like his curly hair and he looks like a little cherub'), Cara herself seemed determined to play it cool. 'I've heard this thing,' she shrugged when pressed for a comment at Topshop's show during London Fashion Week. 'I'm not going to answer this question. I keep my private life private, and that's all I'm going to say.'

Actions, however, speak louder than words, and Harry's presence at the Burberry show several days later only intensified the gossip. Seated in the front row, Harry couldn't seem to take his eyes off Cara as she sashayed down the catwalk. Later on, he had nothing but praise

'Harry is smart and savvy enough not to need a protector. He's probably wiser and more clued up than me. He's conquered America and all that . . . he's like, "I've just played Madison Square Garden, so I'm fine for advice, thanks."'

– Nick Grimshaw

for her appearance. 'She was great,' starry-eyed Harry told an ITN reporter. 'She did a good job. She looked amazing.' As for the clothes on display, Harry said: 'I thought the collection was really amazing. I've always been a fan of Burberry. The colours are nice and subtle, they aren't too much and they're easy to wear.'

According to *The Sun*, however, Cara's management were less than impressed to learn of her famous new admirer. Concerned that Harry's image was 'wrong' for a model of Cara's standing, they supposedly set about warning her off the 1D heartthrob. 'They believe that being linked with Harry could damage her high-end jobs. They want her to stay out of the papers,' an insider told *The Sun*. 'But if anything it's just made Harry more keen. Telling two young people "no" is just going to make them want to meet up even more.'

Harry refused to comment on the story, but when *Look* magazine claimed he'd given Cara a key to his flat, he decided enough was enough. 'The thing is, I do have friends, and I'd say more than 90 per cent of the people I get linked to are friends,' he told *Now*. 'At the moment, it appears I have, like 7,000 girlfriends. It's ridiculous. I think it's crazy. It does get in the way if I like someone. I'll say, "I like you," and they'll say, "But what about this and that?" I have to tell them it's not true. But it gets a bit tiring too.'

Of course, for all those hoping to be the future Mrs Styles, it pays to remember this one simple piece of advice: 'The fun part is the chase, so if you speak to me, play a bit hard to get,' Harry told *Top Of The Pops* magazine. 'I think it's attractive when someone turns you down. You don't want someone to say "yes" straight away, do you?' He was also careful to play down his reputation for being a shameless womaniser: 'I think you have to be cool to be a good flirt – and I don't think I'm very cool.' Yet in another interview he contradicted himself, saying: 'Sometimes I flirt without meaning to. Perhaps it's just how I was meant to be. I've got a good seduction routine which I execute very well. I'm eighteen. I don't love older women – I just love women.'

Generating almost as many headlines as Harry's would-be girlfriends was his growing collection of body art, the latest additions being a tiny 'A' for Anne – inked in the crook of his elbow – and a line from Temper Trap's song, 'Sweet Disposition'. ('Won't stop 'till we surrender,' reads the swirly script beneath a star on Harry's arm.) The man responsible, tattooist Kevin Paul, told *Sugarscape* that Harry was planning on getting a half-sleeve done to cover the upper part of his left arm. When quizzed as to the hidden meanings of Harry's many tatts, however, Paul remained tight-lipped. 'They're really personal to him – the reasons he had them done and stuff,' explained Harry's trusted tattooist, 'so he doesn't really want to announce what they are.'

Kevin, who counts Ed Sheeran and JLS hunk Aston Merrygold among his clients, revealed that Ed is actually responsible for a couple of Harry's less obvious inkings. '[Ed] did a little locket on Harry's hand, like a little padlock thing. They didn't really have to stop because of the pain, it was all pretty small things really so didn't take too long.'

While Kevin has the honour of inking Harry on this side of the pond, whenever he's over in LA, Harry usually drops by the Shamrock Social Club tattoo parlour to check out their designs. It was here that he had Gemma's name etched in Hebrew on his left shoulder, and more recently had two matching swallows inked onto his pecs. On the subject of his latest,

'The fun part is the chase, so if you speak to me, play a bit hard to get. You don't want someone to say "yes" straight away, do you?'
– *Harry Styles*

slightly retro choice, Harry had this to say. 'I like that kind of style of tattoos,' he explained in *US Weekly*, 'like the old sailor kind of tattoos. They symbolise travelling and we travel a lot.' Etched in gorgeous detail, the twin birds are Harry's most detailed pieces yet. But the 1D heartthrob still doesn't seem entirely comfortable going under the needle. 'Anyone who said tattoos don't hurt is a liar,' he laughed.

Tattoos are, of course, for keeps: an almost indelible form of self-expression. And someone perfectly placed to understand the strain of struggling to express himself is former Take That songster, Robbie Williams. 'It's only natural a lad in a boy band will be compared to me,' he told *The Sun*. 'At his age, I was in this lilywhite boy band, Take That. But I was meeting up with mates, jumping out of the tour bus and into a Transit van at motorway service stations all around the country. Whenever I had the chance to go clubbing, I went. It's not a secret anymore, but I would get off my face and have complete anonymity. No one had a camera phone so I could go and enjoy myself properly. Harry is finding out it's not so easy for him.'

Even at the wedding of his friend James Corden, Harry's actions were not free from scrutiny. The guest list at the star-studded reception – held at Babington House, Somerset – included plenty of British celebrities. Yet despite all the classic comics in attendance, best man Ben Winston scored the biggest laugh of the night. James' dubious boy-band past is no secret, and mischievous Ben not only fixed it for his former bandmates to record a cheeky spoof of one of James' old songs, he also persuaded Sir Paul McCartney, Robbie Williams, Gary Barlow, Gary Lightbody and the boys of 1D to get in on the act.

Niall and Louis' matching suits also inspired more than a few giggles. 'We must be spending far too much time together,' Niall quipped. 'It's not like they are similar, they are identical,' added a red-faced Louis. 'We look like Jedward!'

'I think you have to be cool to be a good flirt – and I don't think I'm very cool.'
– *Harry Styles*

'The worst thing about living with Harry is the constant stream of girls he is getting through our door – it's relentless!'
- Louis Tomlinson

But none of their high jinx were enough to take the focus off of Harry, who came down to breakfast the following morning with none other than gorgeous songstress Natalie Imbruglia. Knowing Harry's reputation with the ladies, their fellow guests naturally put two and two together. When quizzed about their supposed hook-up, Natalie responded sharply, 'Why are you asking me? Go ask him.' Comedian Alan Carr did as much on his late-night show, yet all Harry had to say was: 'We were at James Corden's wedding. We'd never met before, and that was literally it [. . .] I guess we kinda left at the same time, so it might have looked a bit dodgy.'

Despite Harry's denials, the media refused to let the rumour lie. And when the boys performed at the iTunes festival at the Roundhouse a few days later, Harry's new pal, Radio One *Breakfast Show* DJ Nick Grimshaw, mischievously added fuel to the fire by tweeting: 'They are doing a cover of "Torn" by Natalie Imbruglia. LOLLLLZZZZ.'

In fact, Harry's bromance with Nick 'Grimmy' Grimshaw was only just beginning. The two were regularly seen out together at all the hippest celebrity hangouts. 'We chatted a bit, and then we kept bumping into each other,' Harry revealed. 'We have the same sense of humour and we come from the same place. His brother's from where my dad lives. [Nick] is just so funny. You can hear it on the radio – he just makes me laugh.'

On 11 August, Harry turned out to celebrate Nick's twenty-eighth birthday at the Groucho Club along with Mark Ronson, Sadie Frost, Jaime Winston, Tulisa and Kate Moss, who – according to *The Sun* – made a beeline for Harry as soon as she spotted him. Perched on his lap, she told him that her daughter Lila was a huge 1D fan. Like any other Directioner, Kate was keen to get a picture of herself with the band's curly-haired singer. Starry-eyed Harry was happy to oblige. 'It's cool with people like Kate,' he told *The Sun*. 'I wouldn't say I was really great mates with her, but it's weird for her to go, when I saw her at the Olympics, "Oh, Harry, come over."'

One beauty who was less keen to be papped with Harry, however, was Caroline Flack. Yet only a week later – at the birthday party of another mutual friend – the pair were spotted chatting happily, suggesting that Caroline's decision to keep her distance at Grimmy's bash was prompted by her need to stay out of the tabloids – and off Directioners' list of potential voodoo victims – rather than any animosity towards Harry.

When Grimmy took over Chris Moyles' *Breakfast Show*, Harry wasted no time in showing his support, calling for Directioners everywhere to tune in to his new BFF. As a reward, Nick intended to debut 'Live While We're Young', but this was not to be. 'The plan was to play [their] latest single,' explained the DJ. 'Then it was leaked and we were like, "Oh . . . but let's talk to them anyway! They really need the push, so they can start doing really well." I originally demanded to talk to them at 7:20am, but their management said it was too early.'

From then on, Harry has made a habit of hanging out in the studio, engaging Grimmy in random topics of conversation. 'I want to shave my hair off,' he announced one morning. 'Everyone's telling me not to do it. I think my popularity is in my face and not my hair. I think it would be fine.' He was also happy to help out with Grimmy's on-air pranks – one of which was hatched against his stylist Caroline Watson. When Caroline picked up the phone, Harry casually told her that, 'I was reading a magazine today and I saw this big article . . . talking about men wearing tights. And I was wondering because, erm, basically, whenever you've got me dressed . . . it just feels really comfortable, so I've been putting them under my jeans. So, I'm just wondering if you can get me some good ones. Like, crotchless ones, because I've been stealing my sister's . . . Do you think they do, like, gold ones?' To the boys' amusement, Caroline fell for it completely, promising Harry she'd get hold of some tights and bring them to their next meeting.

As always, Harry had other women on his mind, namely the pretty *Made In Chelsea* 'It' girl Caggie Dunlop. Though the two had been friends since the previous spring – when Caggie playfully replied to Harry's tweets with the question, 'do you want to come over?' and 'I love Harry Styles' – their first real meeting (at a party close to Harry's London pad) hadn't quite lived up to the flirtatious banter. Though they spent the entire evening in each other's company, nothing – other than a kiss and a cuddle – happened, perhaps due to Harry's 1D commitments (the boys were about to embark on the US leg of the Up All Night Tour). They did, however, keep in touch via text while Harry was away. Things went quiet again while Harry was dating Caroline, but over recent weeks he'd got back in touch.

'For me the Olympics literally can't be topped. Just the feeling of being in that room, all our families were there . . . it was unbelievable.'

– *Harry Styles*

The sight of them partying together at South Kensington's exclusive club, Dorsia, was more than enough to set tongues wagging, especially since Caggie, who is five years older than Harry, had jokingly told *The Sun* that she liked the idea of finding a younger man. She later backtracked, insisting she and Harry were just friends – but to no avail. The Twitter trolls already had Caggie in their sights. 'It was horrible for Caggie,' her *Made In Chelsea* co-star Millie Mackintosh told *Marie Claire*. 'I'm not going to speak about it, but when people are turning up outside your parents' house it's gone too far. Caggie is a fun-loving girl . . . but it does all get a bit much.'

Luckily Caggie's on-off boyfriend Spencer Matthews was happy to set the record straight. Having bonded with Harry over a shared love of pocket handkerchiefs ('he was asking my advice on . . . whether to go for a square or a more voluminous option,' he revealed in *Heat* magazine), Spencer found himself wondering what Harry was like in bed. When he'd quizzed Millie on the subject, she'd retorted simply, 'I don't know.'

Despite getting to know the *MIC* crew, Harry was spending more and more time with Nick Grimshaw. Given the age gap – Grimmy is ten years older – this is yet another relationship in Harry's life that's come under serious scrutiny. 'Some people latch on to and become friends with celebrities,' mused BBC funnyman Russell Howard in an interview with *The Sun*. 'It's so odd. The one that intrigues me is Nick Grimshaw hanging out with Harry Styles. Like, Nick is my age and Harry is about eighteen and they play Frisbee together – it's rather weird. How have they become best buddies?' Was Grimmy harbouring a secret crush on the 1D hottie? Much to his amusement, Harry has been the butt of jokes about his sexuality ever since he and Louis first became roomies. Far from denying the rumours, he's gone out of his way to play up to them. In interview with *Top Of The Pops* he playfully confessed that out of all his 1D bandmates he'd 'go out with Liam because he's a genuine, kind-hearted boy'.

Another theory is that Nick is simply using Harry to bolster the flagging ratings of his *Breakfast Show*. But this seems equally nonsensical. After all, there's more to Harry than his handsome face – as Nick himself pointed out in an interview with *Heat*. 'I don't feel protective [towards Harry],' explained the DJ. 'He's smart and savvy enough not to need a protector. He's probably wiser and more clued up about things than me. He's conquered America and all that, and I'm like, "Let me tell you about the time I DJ'ed in Milton Keynes." [. . .] He's like, "I've just played Madison Square Garden, so I'm fine for advice, thanks."'

Yet, Harry himself would beg to differ. Having outgrown his East-End pad, the 1D party-boy was seeking something more palatial, ideally in Primrose Hill – the same glamorous district of London where Grimmy has his studio flat. After several viewings, Harry finally settled on a stucco-fronted four-bed mansion set in lush green gardens and surrounded by high walls – all of which would help to keep his celebrity parties private.

From then on, it was simply a case of choosing the décor – with the assistance of his über-cool new neighbour, Kate Moss. Amongst Harry's new purchases were a print of Rihanna by the up-and-coming graffiti artist Bambi and another of Kate Moss by Banksy. Together the prints are rumoured to have set Harry back £100,000. Yet while money was no object, he still knew the value of the pieces he'd acquired. 'My dad's a financial advisor, so that helps,' he told *Fabulous* magazine. 'He's always said to me, "For every £10 you make, say you spend £7 of it wisely, the other £3 it doesn't matter what you do."' So having made two wise purchases, Harry thought nothing of splurging £23,000 on a jewel-encrusted Audemars Piguet watch.

Having tasted success beyond their wildest dreams with *Up All Night* (already certified multi-platinum), Harry and the boys had entered the studio to begin work on the follow-up with a huge weight of expectation on their shoulders. Yet when it came to beating the dreaded 'second-album syndrome', 1D had a strategy all their own. 'We didn't want to

> ### 'I want to shave my hair off. Everyone's telling me not to do it . . . I think it would be fine.'
> #### – Harry Styles

change it up too much. We wanted to keep it quite similar, but make a few subtle differences,' Niall revealed. 'As we've got older we want the music to grow up with us the songs are about things that have happened in our own experiences.'

In fact, the boys had started working on the album that would become *Take Me Home* back in May at Stockholm's Kinglet Studios. On tour in the States, they fitted in sessions at Chalice Studios, LA, and MixStar Studios, Virginia Beach, whenever possible, before giving the final thirteen tracks a polish at Wendy House Productions in Shepherds Bush. They also journeyed out to Jake Gosling's Sticky Studios in Windlesham, Surrey, where they recorded two numbers – 'Little Things' and 'Over Again' – generously donated by Ed Sheeran. 'I've got two . . . old songs that were meant to go on my last album – a big stadium anthem,' Ed told *Dose.ca*. 'So I'm going to put them towards them and see if they like them, I wouldn't necessarily do that with any other bands.'

McFly's contribution consists of the song 'I Would'. 'It's quite a selective process writing for other bands,' Tom Fletcher told *The Daily Star*. 'I don't want to write a song for just anyone. I only do it for people I really like because that's when you do your best work, so I hope the relationship with One Direction can continue.'

For Tom, 'What Makes You Beautiful' was a veritable 'breath of fresh air'. But, released on Friday 9 November, *Take Me Home* hit the UK's music scene like a force-five hurricane. Over the weekend some 94,000 fans did what the album's title asked. Before the week was out, a further 60,000 copies had flown off the shelves, ensuring the album slammed straight onto the chart at Number One. The album was also sitting pretty atop seventeen other charts around the world. But, if possible, this achievement was topped by news that *Take Me Home* had emulated *Up All Night* in debuting at Number One on the *Billboard* 200, proving lightning can indeed strike the same place twice – especially if One Direction are involved!

Chapter Six

TROUBLE IN PARADISE

*'I think I've been unlucky in love so far . . .
I haven't really met anyone who's made the
earth move for me.'*
– Harry Styles

Harry's secret love of chick flicks – *The Notebook* and *Love Actually* are two of his all-time favourites – reveals more than a little about his priorities in life. 'I wish I had a girl to cuddle up to at night rather than my pillow,' Harry once sighed in an interview with *Twist*. 'I don't mind getting a black eye or a broken arm for a girl as long as she's there to kiss it after.' Fortunately, Harry had more to look forward to at the end of 2012 than the release of a record-breaking new album.

At last it seemed as though 1D's resident matchmaker – 'Harry is the magic match-up man,' Liam once joked. 'When I got with my girlfriend, Harry was the boy who set us up. And with Louis Tomlinson and Eleanor Calder, it was also Harry' – had bagged his very own dream girl. Loyal, funny and precisely the sort of girl you'd want to take home to your parents, she also happened to be pop royalty: one of the few female artists more famous in the States than Harry himself. Indeed, Directioners the whole world over were devastated to learn that Harry's new girlfriend was none other than pretty US pop princess Taylor Swift.

From their first meeting in March, backstage at the Nickelodeon Kids' Choice Awards, Harry is said to have been smitten. As for Taylor – who spent the whole of 1D's performance dancing along and fanning herself – cheeky idol Justin Bieber was on hand to drop a hint as to her feelings for the 1D cutie. 'I already know one of the biggest artists in the world thinks Harry is so hot, but I have been sworn to secrecy,' he teased. However, with Taylor's career running parallel to Harry's – she too was preparing for the release of a new album, the stunning *Red* – the chances of their ever finding the time to get to know each other better appeared remote at best.

Still, impulsive Harry made sure to leave with her number. 'She's a really lovely girl. Honestly, she couldn't be a sweeter person,' he gushed of Taylor later that summer (in *Seventeen*). 'She's a great girl, and she's extremely talented. She's one of those people you meet [who's] genuinely a nice person. Some people you meet and they are not as nice as you make them out to be. But she's one of those people who's really just amazing.'

Incredibly, the media failed to read the signs (still convinced that Cara Delevingne was the only girl for Mr Styles), so were caught looking the other way when *The Sun* revealed that Harry and Taylor were spotted holding hands backstage at the *X Factor USA* studio in LA in November. 'Harry turned up at rehearsals to watch Taylor. She delayed [her performance] for twenty minutes to wait for him,' a studio insider told the paper. 'He was sitting with her mum Andrea and she seemed won over too. After Taylor finished, he picked her up over his shoulder and carried her to her trailer. They were holding hands and flirting all day. They had matching chains on and queued up together to get their lunches from the catering truck. It was all really sweet.'

The show's host Mario Lopez wasted little time in alerting the outside world as to what was happening. 'Taylor Swift was the special guest performer and [here's] a little inside scoop for you. During rehearsals, Harry from One Direction came and slapped me on the back, and said: "Hey, Mario, how ya doing?" And I said, "What are you doing here?" And he sort of pointed towards Taylor. They walked off hand in hand. So Taylor Swift and Harry from One Direction – you heard it here first. [They're] officially hanging out, I can say that much.'

What neither Mario, nor anyone else knew – except for those close to Harry, of course – was that he and Taylor had first gotten together within days of meeting at the Nickelodeon bash, and that Taylor had called time on their romance after photos appeared in the press of Harry in a clinch with Emma Ostilly while One Direction were in New Zealand. Taylor was said to be

> 'I don't mind getting a black eye or a broken arm for a girl as long as she's there to kiss it after.'
> – Harry Styles

heartbroken on seeing Harry in the arms of another girl after supposedly swearing his undying love. 'Taylor really liked Harry,' a source close to her told *Radar Online*. 'Even though they weren't exclusive, he [Harry] had hinted at making it official with her just before he took off for Australia. He even told Taylor he didn't want her seeing anybody else while he was away.'

According to another of Taylor's friends, Taylor had been nervous about giving Harry a second chance. 'Taylor is very full-on in relationships and falls for people quickly,' the friend revealed. 'Harry is being careful because he doesn't want to hurt her again. But he's made it clear that he likes her a lot. They have been seeing each other again for a little while now.'

Of course, with a string of high-profile exes, including squeaky-clean Disney star Joe Jonas, *Twilight* hunk Taylor Lautner, bad-boy rocker John Mayer, and *Jarhead* star Jake Gyllenhaal, Taylor was no stranger to heartbreak. In the aftermath of Harry's fling Down Under, Taylor briefly dated Conor Kennedy, the grandson of Senator Robert Kennedy, and great-nephew of President John F. Kennedy. As with Harry, Conor was several years younger than Taylor, and a friend of Conor's told *The Daily Mail* that politically-minded Taylor was 'more obsessed with the idea of dating a Kennedy, than the actual Kennedy she was dating'. And perhaps Taylor's summer romance was nothing more than a brief distraction from her issues with Harry.

Having grown up in the spotlight, Taylor is only too accustomed to having every aspect of her personal life pored over by the press. The only question was whether Harry himself was up for the challenge of dating a girl more high-profile than himself. 'If you are threatened by some part of what I do and want to cut me down to size in order to make it even – that won't work,' Taylor stated in an interview with *Harper's Bazaar*. 'Also I can't deal with someone who's obsessed with privacy. People kind of care if there are two famous people dating . . . if you care about privacy to the point where we need to dig a tunnel under this restaurant so

'I wish I had a girl to cuddle up to at night rather than my pillow.'
– *Harry Styles*

that we can leave, I can't do that. I like a man to take control. It needs to be equal. If I feel too much like I'm wearing the pants, I start to feel uncomfortable and we break up.'

Either way 'Haylor', as the hot new couple came to be known, were soon back together and all but inseparable. Papped on a string of cute dates around NYC (the loved-up pair were spotted watching sea lions and cooing over a friend's baby in Central Park Zoo), 1D's Harry had plenty to smile about. On 3 December, the boys played their first storming gig at NYC's iconic Madison Square Garden. Of course, it was a sell-out and the boys' families and girlfriends (except for Niall, who was single) all jetted over to support them on the night.

Streets away at Penn Plaza, a pop-up store called '1D World' opened its doors, selling an array of adorable T-shirts, hoodies, hats, onesies, dolls, bracelets, necklaces and phone cases. For $30, Directioners could even walk away with a life-size cardboard cut-out of Harry. Those who simply couldn't be satisfied with a copy set up camp in the Rockefeller Plaza five days ahead of the boys' appearance on the *Today* show on 1 December. Of course, this wouldn't be the first time 1D had brought the plaza and surrounding streets to a standstill. Rather than risk a repeat of the mania, security guards set about handing out numbered orange wristbands to the lucky girls at the front of the queue – along with strict instructions to pack up and return at 2:00am, when they'd finally be able to reclaim their places.

Any Directioners able to tune into the show were treated to three of their favourite tracks: 'What Makes You Beautiful', 'Live While We're Young', and 'Little Things'. After they'd performed the final number, Harry was sure to thank all the fans for their support, not least

'Harry is the magic match-up man – he can do it for everyone else but not himself. He will end up a lonely old man.'
– Liam Payne

those New Yorkers who'd been left homeless in the wake of Hurricane Sandy. 'I think in spite of everything that's happened, our thoughts and prayers are with everyone that's been affected by Hurricane Sandy,' he said. 'And to see everyone come out still when everything's happened is absolutely amazing. It means so much to us.'

With the 20,000 tickets to the hottest show the Big Apple had hosted in many a year having sold out in less than a minute, it wasn't surprising to find the streets surrounding the venue teeming with excited fans hours in advance of the doors opening, the expectancy cranking ever higher as show-time approached. The reviewer from *Entertainment Weekly* had taken a seat early to sample the atmosphere: 'At one point a teen behind me screamed her brains out and then shrieked, "I don't even know why I'm screaming!!!"' the reviewer said. 'I didn't know either [as] One Direction was not scheduled to take the stage for another hour.' *The New York Daily News* compared the collective scream as the boys came out onto the runway stage and launched into 'Up All Night' as being 'louder than a jet engine, with a pitch higher than a banshee's wail'.

Earlier in the day, Manhattan had played host to a global One Direction fan convention, and seeing the array of flags from countries around the globe proved overwhelming for the boys. Some of the naughtier fans had brought rather more personal items than their homeland's national flag, and Harry found himself pelted with assorted knickers and bras whenever he danced within range. The enormity of what he and the boys were about to do hit Harry backstage, and before going out he let his feelings be known via his Twitter page: 'Thinking about what we were doing three years ago today . . . Today we play Madison Square Garden. We can never thank you enough. We love you xx.' And that wasn't Harry's final tweet for the day. Sensitive Mr Styles even made time to answer his fans' tweets whilst

> 'Taylor is a really lovely
> girl. Honestly, she couldn't
> be a sweeter person.'
> – Harry Styles

live on stage. Adding new meaning to the phrase 'save the best for last', each boy set about hurling autographed papers into the crowd before bursting into the final song of the evening, 'What Makes You Beautiful': the perfect end to a perfect gig . . . and a fabulous year for One Direction themselves.

Even after the show, 1D were determined to continue the party across town at the Hudson Hotel where they'd arranged a karaoke bash for all their family and friends. Taylor (rocking a little black dress to die for) had arrived at Madison Square Garden solo. But at the party, Harry seized his chance to introduce his new love to his mum, dad and stepdad, Robin. With the formalities over, Harry playfully hoisted Taylor into the air, recreating the famous lift scene from *Dirty Dancing*, before joining Ed Sheeran on stage for a dodgy duet of Elton John and Kiki Dee's hit, 'Don't Go Breaking My Heart' (with Ed taking care of the high notes), while Taylor cheered them on. Ed, of course, had got the MSG crowd rocking with a short four-song set, and had also joined the boys on stage to provide back-up vocals on 'Little Things'.

Though she was due in the studio next morning, Taylor partied with her beau well into the early hours. Harry had a free day, but was waiting for Taylor when she returned to her hotel after the recording session. On Wednesday, he was back on 1D duty with an appearance on *The Late Show With David Letterman*, where they shared the sofa with Hollywood heavyweight Dustin Hoffman and performed 'Little Things'. Later that evening, Harry and Taylor enjoyed a romantic dinner date before heading over to the Crosby Street Hotel, where Taylor introduced Harry to several of her closest girlfriends – all of whom gave Harry their seal of approval.

On 7 December, Harry and the boys returned to Madison Square Garden for the star-studded Z-100 Jingle Ball, where they appeared alongside Taylor, Justin Bieber, and their old *X Factor* housemate, Cher Lloyd. While clowning around on the red carpet with a sprig of mistletoe, Harry was quizzed as to the nature of his relationship with Ms Swift. 'I just bumped into her at the zoo . . . and then I don't know,' he teased before making another fan's Christmas by inviting her to join him under the mistletoe.

Back at London's O2 Arena, 1D was set to appear at the Capital FM Jingle Bell Ball. However, rather than fly home with the boys, Harry opted for a seat on Taylor's private jet. With Taylor watching from the VIP suite, Harry and the boys – casually dressed in jeans and T-shirts – got the crowd going with 'C'mon C'mon'. As the tune faded, Harry's sexy Northern accent was enough to send the crowd wild. 'It feels great to back in the UK! You guys are amazing,' he shouted above the din. 'Thank you for having us. Let's have a bit of fun, shall we?'

The festive fun continued with 1D performing 'Kiss You' (their upcoming single) at that year's *X Factor* Final (held at the Manchester Central Arena on 9 December). After the show was done, Harry whisked Taylor straight up to his parents' in Holmes Chapel, where he introduced her to big sister Gemma. He also took his girl to Great Budsworth for a taste of his favourite honeycomb ice cream and dinner at the George & Dragon. On Taylor's twenty-third birthday (13 December), they took a romantic trip to Bowness-on-Windermere. Strolling hand-in-hand through the beautiful lakeside village, they stopped off to feed the doves and swans, en route to Beatrix Potter World.

Of course, no birthday would be complete without presents, and Harry showered his girl with handbags from Burberry and Jimmy Choo (with price tags of £995 and £400

'Harry really likes Taylor, he's fallen for her in a big way . . .
At first, I wasn't sure if the relationship was a real one,
but I talk to him a lot and it seems to be that
she's the one for him – for now, anyway.'
– Nick Grimshaw

respectively), gorgeous antique earrings and a vintage photo-frame containing a black-and-white photograph of himself and Taylor. He also surprised her with 23 cupcakes, specially ordered from the Custom Cupcake Company.

The following day was taken up with a walk through the Peak District, and a celebratory meal with Gemma and her boyfriend at the Styles' local, the Rising Sun in Hope Valley. When the time came for them to part (Taylor was recording in Germany), Harry drove her to Manchester airport, where her private jet was waiting to carry her away. After saying their goodbyes, Harry drove down to Sheffield University, where some pals of his were throwing a party. Needless to say, he was the centre of attention the moment he got out of his car. Though he was happy to pose for photos with various admirers, there was only one woman on his mind. 'Harry really likes Taylor, he's fallen for her in a big way,' his pal Grimmy told *The Mirror*. 'At first, I wasn't sure if the relationship was a real one, but I talk to him a lot and it seems to be that she's the one for him – for now, anyway.'

Harry and Taylor were not to be reunited until after the final of *X Factor* USA (held on 20 December in LA), where 1D performed 'Kiss You' in front of a pair of giant shiny red lips. While in town, Harry couldn't resist a visit to the Shamrock Social Club tattoo parlour. Taylor came along for support and was papped playing pool while her beau had his left bicep inked with a sketch of Nelson's mighty flagship, *HMS Victory*.

Of course, Harry is not the only 1D hottie with a penchant for body art – an interest that was soon to land them in hot water with hordes of irate parents. 'Have a real #1D tattoo?' the boys posted, urging Directioners to 'Show us! Submit a 90 sec YouTube video and show us why you should be in the @1D3Dmovie.' Within minutes they had racked up a staggering 4,000 retweets and 6,000 likes. Yet, the boys had forgotten a single crucial detail: it's illegal

for anyone under the age of eighteen in the UK to get a tattoo. Fearful that many fans would go to any lengths to get closer to the prize – even if it meant breaking the law – the boys opted to do the responsible thing and remove the post immediately.

With his 1D commitments for 2012 officially over, Harry was free to fly with Taylor to Nashville. Having already charmed Taylor's mum, Andrea, he was keen to meet the rest of her family. Though they got on well, Taylor's dad Scott reportedly took Harry aside for a man-to-man chat. A protective father, he didn't want to see his daughter's heart broken all over again. '[Scott] likes Harry, but he wants them to slow down and take things easy,' a source told *The Sun On Sunday*. 'It's clear to everyone they are smitten with one another and are already talking about marriage. He doesn't want them to split up.'

From Nashville, Harry and Taylor headed off on a romantic mini-break at the Canyons Ski Resort, Park City. While they were there, they hooked up with Justin Bieber and his girlfriend, Selena Gomez. While showing off his skills on the slope, Harry fell head over heels in more ways than one, resulting in a mystery chin injury. Though he later posted a picture of his bandaged chin online, 'chin chinnigan, chin chinnigan,' was literally all he had to tweet on the subject. After the holiday, Taylor was bound for Australia, whilst Harry headed back to Cheshire to spend Christmas with his family. Though thousands of miles apart, they kept in touch via cute messages and conversations on Skype. Apparently Harry even serenaded his girl with a romantic singagram. Once again, Harry selected a vintage Christmas present

'I asked for
socks and
pants for
Christmas,
because if
you're out on
the road
you always
run out.'
– *Harry Styles*

for his love in the form of an antique emerald bracelet, while Taylor – knowing Harry's passion for Beatles memorabilia – splurged over £50,000 on rare autographed items. As for his family, generous Harry showered them with expensive gifts, but kept his own wish-list relatively simple. 'I asked for socks and pants for Christmas,' he revealed in an interview with MTV, 'because if you're out on the road you always run out.'

As Taylor was set to perform in Times Square on New Year's Eve, Harry spent Boxing Day with his dad and Olly Murs at Old Trafford, watching their beloved Manchester United play, before jumping on a plane to NYC. Things didn't go according to plan, however, since speedy Styles forgot to pack his passport. A courier was despatched from Holmes Chapel, but not soon enough. Having missed his flight, Harry was left to kick his heels around Manchester airport's VIP lounge for several hours. Arriving at JFK behind schedule, Harry went straight from the airport to a Coldplay and Jay Z gig at Brooklyn's Barclays Centre, before dashing over the bridge to Times Square like a dutiful boyfriend.

Along with Big Ben, Times Square has a reputation as one of the most exciting places in the world to welcome in the New Year, and as the clock struck midnight that night, Harry pulled Taylor close for a fairytale kiss – to the crowd's delight. The very next day, however, the couple had plans to swap NYC for the Caribbean, jetting off for a romantic break on Virgin Gorda.

According to an island insider, the sun-soaked vacation was about more than just fun in the sun. 'Taylor really wants [her and Harry] to stand the test of time, but she doesn't see how it could work if they weren't at least in the same country,' the insider told *Reveal* of Taylor's secret anxieties. 'Taylor has fallen for Harry big time but she's realistic enough to know they may not last if it's a long-distance relationship. She keeps telling Harry she can't bear being apart from him, and he's so smitten with her that he's already started looking at ways to make moving to America work. Harry's so mad about her that he'll do anything to keep her happy, and if moving to the US is what it takes to show her he's in the relationship for keeps, he will make the move.'

However, the only move Harry ended up making was to neighbouring Necker Island (owned by Virgin tycoon Richard Branson) following an 'almighty bust-up' with Taylor over his lack of commitment. Less than 24 hours after the loved-up pair were papped enjoying a candlelit dinner by the sea (Harry sporting his trademark beanie despite the heat), claustrophobic Harry was reportedly seeking some alone-time. '[Harry] got drunk and left Taylor on their boat for a few hours without telling her where he was going,' revealed *US Weekly*'s mystery source. By the time her wayward boyfriend returned, tearful Tay had knocked back more than a few drinks herself and was said to be 'furious'. The same source heard her calling Harry a 'd***' and yelling angrily that he was 'lucky' to even be with her. 'Taylor knows she's far more high-profile in America and way richer, and saw her career as more important,' the insider added. 'She always brushed off his schedule and needs and put hers first.'

'Taylor has serious trust issues, something that is being severely tested dating Harry,' the source added. 'Harry courts a lot of attention. He's a big flirt and loves the ladies. Taylor doesn't like that . . . She thought he was cheating on her when they were apart over the holidays so she ended it, telling him she couldn't be in a relationship with someone like that.'

Harry supposedly pleaded innocent to the charges, but by then Taylor wasn't listening. '[Harry's] reputation precedes him and it's hard to believe Taylor will ever be able to fully trust Harry because the ladies just throw themselves at him and he does nothing to temper that.' Whatever the truth, a picture speaks a thousand words. Hours after his split with Taylor, Harry was papped in a hot tub on Necker Island, eating gourmet sushi, sipping champagne and splashing around with a pretty blonde presenter named Hermione Way.

As for Taylor, she opted to catch the next plane home to the States on 4 January – a full three days before the couple had planned to leave. Pictured on a boat at Virgin Gorda's US Customs, the songstress cut a lonely figure. 'Til you put me down,' she tweeted sadly at the end of the holiday (a line from her single, 'Trouble'). After just 65 days, it seemed the whirlwind romance was officially over.

Visibly downcast, Harry returned to London a couple of days later to help promote the video for 'Kiss You' – which featured the boys larking around on skis, motorbikes and dressed in sexy matching sailor suits. The single had been released as a digital download back in November, and was riding high in charts on both sides of the Atlantic. Premiered worldwide on Vevo on 7 January, the teaser clip alone scored a staggering 10.4 million views in 24 hours. Indeed, there was no chance of Harry being left to brood on his recent love split. With a 118-date world tour on the horizon (in support of *Take Me Home*), Harry had more than enough to occupy his thoughts for the next seven months. On the road with four mates who've always had his best interests at heart, he couldn't have been in better company. In happier times, Taylor and Harry would surely have discussed the upcoming People's Choice Awards, slated for 9 January in LA, since both she and 1D were up for awards. As it was, Taylor arrived at the Nokia Theater alone and came away with Favourite Country Artist. As for 1D, they scored not one but two awards: Favourite Song ('What Makes You Beautiful') and Favourite Album (*Up All Night*). Though Harry and the boys were unable to attend, they sent their heartfelt thanks via video.

> 'Thinking about what we were doing three years ago today . . . Today we play Madison Square Garden. We can never thank you enough.'
>
> – Harry Styles

As two of the hottest artists in the world, there was no avoiding each other forever. In fact, 1D and Taylor were set to come face-to-face at the NRJ Music Awards in Cannes on 27 January, where both were due to perform: 'Kiss You' (1D) and 'I Knew You Were Trouble' (Taylor) – a song that's rumoured to have been inspired by Taylor's initial tryst with Harry in April. However, in the build-up to the awards, news broke that Harry and Taylor had had a heart to heart over the phone and decided to give their relationship another go. A source close to Taylor told *The Sun*: 'Taylor realised she was being a bit full-on. She is now more relaxed about their relationship. She intends to enjoy it more rather than worry about where it could eventually lead. Harry is not the sort of guy you can stay mad at for long. She's given him some space and it's done them both a world of good. What happened over New Year is now a distant memory.'

Written across Harry's face, however, was a different story; papped the moment he touched down in Nice, handsome Harry was looking thoroughly miserable. And indeed, rumours of any rekindled romance proved groundless. But, while Taylor – who stole the show in a jewelled gown by Elie Saab – returned to the US solo, it wasn't all bad news for Harry, as One Direction scooped the award for Best International Group.

By his nineteenth birthday, Harry seemed to be back to his usual fun-loving self. On 1 February, he opted to mark the occasion with a raucous bash at Rita's Bar & Dining Room in Dalston, East London, where he treated forty lucky guests – including Niall and best pals Grimmy and Pixie Geldof – to a slap-up meal of fried chicken and duck wings washed down with frozen margaritas, Jägerbombs, beer, wine and champagne. Harry's surprise present – courtesy of Grimmy – was a raunchy lap dance from a striking brunette dressed in a saucy

WPC outfit. Photos taken that evening show Harry grinning from ear-to-ear as the girl gyrated between his legs and playfully slapped him with her truncheon. 'It lasted about ten minutes, but the girl stayed after and chatted to guests,' a source told *The Sunday Mirror*. 'She took her clothes off but kept her bra and pants on.'

After the meal, the party moved to the Alibi club, where Harry reportedly splurged another £3,500 on drinks before passing out on a sofa at 6:00am. 'He was really, really happy,' the source said. 'He was pretty drunk and looked like he was enjoying himself.' Harry himself had this to say: '[It was a] great night. I was in stitches, it was really funny . . . unfortunately there was a no-nudity policy in the bar.'

Fast-forward to the 2013 BRIT Awards (held at London's O2 Arena on 19 February) and all eyes were on Haylor once again. Indeed, Taylor had already given the tabloids plenty to write about. Midway through performing her hit break-up jam 'We Are Never Ever Getting Back Together' at the Grammys nine days earlier, the songstress couldn't resist taking a dig at her boy-bander ex. 'So he calls me up and he's like, "I still love you," and I'm like, "I'm sorry. I'm busy opening the Grammys and we are never, ever getting back together,"' Swift deadpanned, adopting a British accent that couldn't possibly belong to any of her other exes.

But if reporters at the star-studded BRIT Awards were hoping for a war of words, then they were to be sorely disappointed. Ever the gentleman, Harry simply stated that, 'Taylor's a great performer and she always performs great. She's been doing it a long time . . . It was just another good Taylor Swift performance.'

Though the boys lost out on Best Group to Mumford & Sons, they did pick up the first-ever Global Success Award for their mighty international sales record – higher than any other UK act in 2012. Meanwhile, Harry's love life was back in the headlines, when the newly-single star turned up at the BBC Radio One studios – where he was set to co-host *The Breakfast Show* with Grimmy – with wannabe model Camilla 'Millie' Brady on his arm. Harry and Millie first hooked up at the Arts Club in Mayfair – the venue for a glitzy BRIT after-party – and she had accompanied him back to Grimmy's flat where they partied till dawn. A source told *The Sun*: 'Nothing actually happened . . . but there was some pretty serious flirting going on. She accompanied Harry and Nick to Radio One to do their show. Harry gave her a tour of the studio, but then Millie had to go to work. She and Harry plan on meeting up at this weekend or next week.'

Though keen to see Millie again, Harry was as busy as ever with the UK leg of 1D's Take Me Home Tour, set to kick off with back-to-back shows at the O2 on 23 February, in front of 20,000 adoring fans. While concerned as to the impact of extra matinee shows on the boys

'I don't look at myself as the Robbie Williams of the band – I don't think that kind of comparison is on any of our minds. I just can't think about life beyond One Direction at the moment. It's going so well and we are like brothers.'
– *Harry Styles*

(added due to overwhelming demand), no critic could fault their performance on opening night. *The Sun* dubbed them '1Derful!' and rightly so. Reviews for their back-to-back Glasgow SECC gigs were equally enthusiastic. The only real complaint came from *brignewspaper.com*: with Directioners' screaming the organisers really should have provided ear-defending plugs.

Harry himself could have benefited from protection of a different sort. At the sight of the 1D heartthrob on stage, one fan got so carried away that she hurled her shoe at him – midway through the boys' Q&A session. Cheeky Harry was clearly amused. He bent to pick up the offending item. 'Why only one?' he quipped, holding the trainer up for all to see. In answer, a second shoe came flying through the air, hitting Harry exactly where it hurts. Though he dropped to the ground in agony, Harry was determined not to let the incident ruin the evening. After picking himself up, he was ready to carry on. The phantom shoe-flinger might well have gotten away with it, had her mother not called a local radio station to confess. 'I just wanted him to touch something belonging to me,' fourteen-year-old Jade told *The Daily Record*. 'I didn't mean to hit him where I hit him; I'm really embarrassed.'

Meanwhile, Harry arranged a second secret date with Millie. Since 1D was playing in Cardiff on 2 March, the pair planned to hook up at Kuku Club later that evening – except that Harry failed to show. Next up were two gigs in Dublin ('welcome home, Niall' tweeted Harry cheekily on 12 March), and one storming show in Manchester (after which hungry Harry couldn't resist giving a shout out to, 'the person eating a kebab . . . You're my hero'). Even after the gig, the boys' work wasn't done. 15 March, after all, marked a special date on 1D's calendar: Red Nose Day. Inspiring crazed antics across the UK, 'Do something funny for money,' is the slogan for this day of fundraising. In 2013, few celebs did more for the cause than Harry and his bandmates.

Back on 17 February, the boys released 'One Way Or Another (Teenage Kicks)'. An insanely catchy mash-up of two different rock anthems (by Blondie and the Undertones), 'One Way . . . ' shot straight to Number One on the UK singles chart, shifting an incredible 113,000 copies in the first week (despite being leaked online beforehand) – not that the

'Harry's reputation precedes him and it's hard to believe Taylor will ever be able to fully trust Harry because the ladies just throw themselves at him and he does nothing to temper that.'

– US Weekly

boys saw a penny of the profits. In fact, they'd pledged all royalties to charity. Featuring the boys' antics on the streets of London (in the company of Prime Minister David Cameron, no less), the filming of the music video also called for a trip to some of the very poorest areas of Ghana. Visiting schools and hospitals around the poverty-stricken city of Accra proved a heart-breaking experience that Harry's unlikely to forget any time soon. Moved to tears by the sight of infants so sick with malaria that they could barely even lift their heads, an emotional Harry told *The Mirror*: 'We all had moments. If you get involved in it and you don't cry you're superhuman. We've seen appeal films before so we thought we knew what it's like. But when you're there and you get the smells, your eyes hurt from the smoke, you cough . . . you're feeling it all.'

Inspired by the incredible spirit of many of the teens he encountered, Harry added, 'The crazy thing is, when I went to school not one person wanted to be there. Yet you go into a school in Ghana and every child loves it. It's amazing to see. There are ten-year-old kids speaking better French than I can. It's crazy how quick you get connections with children and people who live there. You feel upset leaving them and saying goodbye to them.'

Appearing live on the BBC's epic fundraising show, Harry was sure to get the party started in style. As the catchy opening riff of 'One Way . . .' kicked in, he could barely keep the cheeky grin from his face – and indeed, it was a good match with his giant pillar-box red nose.

The following night (16 March) it was back to business with two more shows at

'If you get involved in it and you don't cry you're superhuman. When you're there and you get the smells, your eyes hurt from the smoke, you cough . . . you're feeling it all.'

– Harry Styles

Manchester's MEN Arena. In between, Harry and the boys found time to watch Man Utd play Reading. Their VIP tickets to the game came courtesy of Harry's new pal Rio Ferdinand. In return, Harry fixed it for the Reds' star to attend not one but two 1D gigs in a row. 'Just at the 1Direction concert,' tweeted 34-year-old Ferdy from inside the MEN. 'Never heard so much screaming!! Lads on fire!' On Saturday, super-fan Harry rocked a replica of Rio's No. 5 jersey live onstage. 'Hope you enjoyed the show tonight @rioferdy5,' he tweeted at the end of the night. To which Rio replied: 'The rolled up shirt sleeve is what I'm doing next game. That's what makes you beautiful.' And the bromance didn't end there. To show his appreciation, Rio fixed it for his exclusive eatery, Rosso, to stay open later than usual, allowing him and the boys to feast on Italian delicacies after hours.

Meanwhile, Harry simply couldn't seem to leave the cougar rumours behind. This time the lady at the heart of the story was Yvette Fielding, mum of his old school mate Will. Bizarrely, the 44-year-old presenter had reportedly claimed to have received flirty text messages from Harry across the table in a Chinese restaurant – with both their families present. Harry would have been just sixteen at the time. Fortunately, both Harry and a mortified Yvette have since denied the rumours. 'The idea that Harry tried to seduce me is, quite frankly, ludicrous,' she told *Heat*. 'We all went for a meal . . . we were all having fun texting funny made-up words to each other. None, and I repeat *none*, were disgusting.'

As for Harry, though he was quick to rubbish it, he took this latest story in his stride.

'I understand why people would wanna know stuff like that,' he shrugged. 'If someone does stuff like that then I wanna know about it too.' Harry's laidback outlook could only be a blessing – particularly with news that the boys would soon be joining the ranks of the über-famous on show at Madame Tussauds.

Wandering the halls of this star-studded London attraction – where waxy doubles of the likes of Michael Jackson, Amy Winehouse and Kylie Minogue remain permanently on show – the bandmates were astonished to learn that they'd be the next young stars to get waxed. 'I'm really just kind of overwhelmed,' wide-eyed Harry told Madame Tussauds' press officer. 'We've been to Madame Tussauds to see the kind of people that get in there . . . it's crazy to think we'll be up there with them,' he added with a smile. Peace-loving Mahatma Ghandi will always be Harry's favourite figure, but when questioned as to who Madame Tussauds should make next, Harry was undeniably stumped. 'Um, I think you should make –' he faltered, before breaking off to add the interviewer: 'who is there not . . . Mother Theresa?' His only concern should certain Directioners want to lock lips with his statue? 'Um, it might get a bit waxy. Maybe they should make 'em out of lip balm.'

That very morning (3 April), *Daybreak* screened an exclusive video clip, showing exactly how 1D came to be immortalised in wax. Ninety minutes and 200 measurements later, the boys emerged from the sculptor's chair covered in measle-like markings but grinning from ear to ear. For all those seeking the next best thing to meeting Harry in the flesh, 1D's gorgeous waxworks were unveiled on 18 April.

Early April also saw the boys return to London for extra shows at the O2. On 6 April, Liam Payne gave 20,000 lucky Directioners a moment they'll remember forever. As Harry began to croon out the romantic solo midway through 'What Makes You Beautiful', cheeky Liam Payne took his chance. Whispering to Louis to hold his mic, he sneakily positioned himself behind his unsuspecting bandmate. One good yank and Harry's black skinny jeans were round his ankles; treating to crowd to a view of the heartthrob's tiny black boxers. If the prank came as a shock then Harry disguised it like a pro. Managing to wrench his jeans back up, he never missed a note.

Of course, messing with Harry on stage has become a hilarious 1D tradition. In Newcastle, it was Louis' turn to get in on the mischief. Perched on a girder at the city's Metro Radio Arena, it was Harry's turn beneath the silvery blue spotlight. 'I'm in love with you,' he crooned softly, during the smooch-inducing 'Little Things'. But before he'd even passed the mic along, Louis spoke the name of Taylor – softly but more than loud enough to set the other boys sniggering.

Midway through the UK tour, it was revealed via the 1D website that the boys were working on a 'shiny new papery volume' called *One Direction, Where We Are: Our Band*

'I like cute girls who are funny. I don't really have a type . . . I do
like girls with short hair, but I also like girls with long hair.'
– *Harry Styles*

Our Story'. To celebrate, Directioners were invited to send in their designs for a One
Direction-inspired national flag. The best submissions stand to win a place in the book itself.

At the time of writing, however, the number one topic among Directioners everywhere
has to be the upcoming 1D3D movie, *This Is Us*, which is set to hit cinemas on 30 August.
The film's director is Morgan Spurlock, aka the man behind *Super Size Me*, a shocking 2004
documentary in which Morgan attempts to live on only McDonald's meals for 30 days. But
if he'd hoped to avoid his own personal food hell on the road with 1D, Morgan was to be
sadly disappointed. 'The boys love eating McD in front of me,' he sighed in interview with
The Independent. '[But] on the new tour they have a trainer who's keeping them off the Big
Macs.' Aside from following the boys on their Take Me Home Tour, the film will also give
the fans telling insights into their personal lives. 'I think fans may shed a tear or two while
watching,' Morgan revealed. 'We spend a lot of down time with the band, with their families
and friends. We really wanted you to see what their "normal" lives are like.'

But that's not all Directioners can expect to see, as Morgan promised: '[There are] more
shirtless moments than you can imagine. Now how many of those make it into the final film
we'll have to wait and see.'

Ever since the boys unveiled their teaser trailer for the movie back on 8 February, the
blogosphere's been positively buzzing with rumours of all the hot gossip contained therein.

A two-minute slice of gorgeousness, showing Harry at work, rest and play – whether it's dancing goofily through a park ('I feel like I'm in a music video,' he laughs), cuddling up to his mum ('no matter how big or famous you get, you'll always be my baby,' Anne assures him), or gleefully watching BFF Louis headbutt a pair of china teacups – the teaser hints at exciting revelations to come – not least the truth about Harry's romance with Taylor Swift. Having branded the country singer a 'pain' in the backside, he's apparently asked for all scenes featuring her to be cut from the movie.

Treated to a sneak peek of the footage, *The Daily Star Sunday* has already hinted at some of the juicier details. 'I haven't met a girl yet who I'd want to even think of getting serious with,' Harry reportedly confides on film. 'I think I've been unlucky in love so far . . . I haven't really met anyone who's made the earth move for me.' Contrary to popular belief, Harry confessed he can't wait to settle down with one special lady. 'I'm longing to meet someone who really inspires me and makes me really want to spend time with them.'

But perhaps Harry is already closer to finding the 'one' than he's letting on. 'Happy end of UK tour to 5secondsofsummer [1D's Aussie tourmates],' tweeted Harry. But between the boys' epic finale in Manchester (20 April) and the first date of the European leg (set to kick off on 29 April at Paris' gargantuan Bercy concert hall), there stretched a full nine days.

'I'm longing to meet someone who really inspires me and makes me really want to spend time with them.'
– Harry Styles

How Harry planned to spend his downtime is still something of a mystery. Rather than hang with his 1D bandmates on the streets of Paris, Harry – after heading home and taking a hammering from his mum on the Scrabble board – opted to jet over to LA alone. Pretty soon, Twitter was flooded with pics of the heartthrob's visit: Harry's shades on a golden beach; Harry schmoozing with celebs at a glam Instagram bash (actress Tori Spelling wasted no time in posting a snap of 'me and my new boyfriend Harry!'). Yet, exactly *what* he was doing in the City of Angels was still unclear. Could Harry be secretly hooking up with a new lady friend? If so, she certainly wouldn't be the first all-American girl Harry has dated.

'Is there any truth behind it all?' *Sugarscape*'s semi-hysterical scribe was dying to know. And she wasn't to be left in suspense for long. On 26 April, Harry was papped exiting Dan Tana's restaurant in Hollywood. He wasn't alone. Earlier that evening he'd been to watch 68-year-old crooner Rod Stewart play the Troubadour. Yet, unlike any other fan in attendance, he'd been invited along for a cosy family dinner afterwards with Rod's wife Penny and daughter Kimberly. Fourteen years older than Harry, it's easy to see how stunning Kimberly 'is exactly Harry's type' (according to *E! News*' source). That the 33-year-old stunner (who's willowy and blonde like Taylor Swift) was papped placing a protective hand on Harry's back as he clambered into the Stewarts' ride home only added fuel to the fire. Of course, only time will tell if the relationship is real, rather than idle tabloid gossip.

Of course, Harry's celebrity status makes keeping a low profile all but impossible. Media and fans were out in force when he arrived at LAX to check-in for the overnight flight to Paris and a similar scene greeted him on arrival at Charles de Gaulle airport, where security was beefed up to keep the excited throng at bay. And after details of where Harry would be staying were leaked on the internet it was inevitable that hundreds of Directioners would be there to meet him outside the appropriately-named Hôtel Amour on Rue Navarin. Harry

didn't seem to mind the attention, however, setting off for a stroll around Montmartre, happily posing for photos and chatting with stunned and delighted fans.

Come the day of the show and those same fans were outside the Paris Bercy arena as soon as it was light in the hope of getting a coveted spot in the front row. During the build-up to showtime, these dedicated Directioners amused themselves by singing the songs they'd be hearing in a few hours' time, while dancing and waving posters bearing the names of their favourite band member. Surely, many of them were dreaming of seeing Harry and the boys springing to life from the posters, so imagine the hysteria when Louis did just that by scaling the arena's sloping, grass-covered walls to give them all a wave from the parapet!

The sell-out 17,000-strong crowd could barely contain themselves as the countdown got underway and when the boys finally came bounding onto the strobe-lit stage the arena erupted into ear-piercing and flashbulb-popping pandemonium. Harry then sent thousands of French girls' hearts a-flutter by addressing them in their native language – 'on s'appelle les One Direction' – before blowing a kiss. Amid shrieks of Je t'aime and Je t'adore, the fans held up lip-shaped sheets of paper they'd each been given on entry to create a sea of crimson kisses.

Just as they had done at every show on the Take Me Home Tour to date, Harry and the boys got their Parisian party started with 'Up All Night', the up-tempo title track from their multi-platinum-selling debut album, which had made One Direction a household name in every corner of the globe. With the exception of 'Gotta Be You', the 24 – song set-list included all the hit singles: 'More Than This', 'One Thing', 'One Way or Another (Teenage Kicks)', 'Little Things', and 'Live While We're Young'. And with songs to suit every mood, even the parents – having repeatedly heard the songs emanating from their daughters' bedrooms – were up on their feet and joining in with the choruses.

'I think you have to take me for me. I am who I am.'
– Harry Styles

Between songs, Harry and the boys took time out for some playful onstage banter, their attempts to converse in schoolbook French provoking further squeals of delight. This was the boys' first concert tour in the country and they marked the occasion with a truly dazzling show. As the performance came to an end, with a final rendition of 'What Makes You Beautiful', thousands of red, white, and blue balloons came cascading down from the ceiling.

After the show, an elated Harry tweeted, *'J'adore la France.'* His French followers responded in kind: *'Nous vous adorons, Harry Styles.'* These sentiments would surely be echoed in many languages in the coming months as One Direction continued their tour across Europe – from Belgium, Germany and Holland, on to Scandinavia and down to Italy, Spain and Portugal on 26 May. On 8 June, the boys were scheduled to return to American shores. In the precious few days between, Harry committed himself to a gig like no other. On 1 June, his mum Anne Cox was set to wed long-term love, Robin, in the quaint UK town of Congleton. Beaming proudly, Harry was delighted to be the one to walk his mother down the aisle. Clad in a dapper tailored suit, he also served as Robin's best man. Seven days later, 1D resumed their epic Take Me Home Tour with dates scheduled in 48 cities across Mexico, the States, Canada, Australia and New Zealand.

What the future holds for Harry Styles is the source of as much speculation as his love life, but one thing's for sure: Harry is riding high with One Direction right now and is in no hurry to go solo just yet. 'I just can't think about life beyond One Direction at the moment,' he says, happily. 'It's all going so well and we are like brothers.' For true Directioners, those words are music to our ears.

British Library Cataloguing in Publication Data
A catalogue record for this book is available from
the British Library

ISBN-13: 978-0-85965-512-5

Cover photo by Camera Press/ Roger Rich
Cover and book design by Coco Wake-Porter
Printed in Great Britain by Bell & Bain Ltd.

Acknowledgements
The author would like to extend professional thanks
to Millie Jones for her painstaking research, and to
Laura Coulman, Sandra Wake, Laura Slater, Tom
Branton and everyone at Plexus. Personal thanks to
Mum, Nan, GD, Sarah, Libby, Sophie, and Thalia.

Harry Styles has given innumerable interviews
to newspapers, magazines, websites, television, and
radio. The author and editors would like to give
special thanks to the following: *Twist*; *Seventeen*;
Harper's Bazaar; *Entertainment Weekly*; *Reveal*;
US Weekly; *Woman*; *Mizz*; *Heat*; *Rolling Stone*;
Billboard; *Look*; *Now*; *Top of the Pops*; *Marie
Claire*; *Fabulous*; *We Love Pop*; *OK!*; *Grazia*;
The Sun; *The Daily Mail*; *New York Daily News*;
The Mirror; *The Sun on Sunday*; *The Sunday
Mirror*; *The Daily Record*; *The Independent*; *The
Independent on Sunday*; *The Daily Star*; *The Daily
Star Sunday*; *The People*; *Wolverhampton Express
& Star*; *The Sunday Times*; (Melbourne) *Herald
Sun*; *ITN News*; *MTV News*; *The X Factor*; BBC
Radio One; radaronline.com; brignewspaper.com;
sugarscape.com; kansascity.com; fanpop.com;
digitalspy.co.uk; stuff.co.nz; 4music.com; dose.ca;
www.madametussauds.co.uk; https://twitter.com/
Harry_Styles; and www.onedirectionmusic.com/gb.

The following books and documentaries proved
invaluable for research purposes: *One Direction: A
Year In The Making*; *Harry Styles: An Unauthorised
Autobiography* by Alice Montgomery; *Harry Styles:
Every Piece Of Me* by Louisa Jepson; *One Direction:
No Limits* by Mick O'Shea; *One Direction: Dare
to Dream: Life as One Direction* by One Direction;
*One Direction: Forever Young: Our Official X
Factor Story* by One Direction.

We would also like to thank the following
agencies for supplying photographs: Fred Duval/
Getty Images; IBL/ Rex Features; Neil Mockford/
FilmMagic/ Getty Images; Kevin Mazur/ Getty
Images; Beretta/ Sims/ Rex Features; McPix Ltd/
Rex Features; Stephen Lovekin/ Getty Images;
Newspix/ Rex Features; Toby Zerna/ Newspix/
Rex Features; Neil Mockford/ FilmMagic/Getty
Images; Beretta/ Sims/ Rex Features; McPix Ltd/
Rex Features; Mike Marsland/ WireImage/ Getty
Images; Rex Images; George Pimentel/ WireImage/
Getty Images; McPix Ltd/ Rex Features; Brian
Rasic/ Rex Features; Fred Duval/ FilmMagic/
Getty Images; Anna Gowthorpe/ PA Archive/ Press
Association Images; Richard Young/ Rex Features;
McPix Ltd/ Rex Features; Sara Jaye/ Rex Features;
Startraks Photo/ Rex Features; Matt Baron/ BEI/
Rex Features; Neilson Barnard/ Getty Images;
Debra L. Rothenberg/ FilmMagic/ Getty Images;
Abaca/ Press Association Images; Richard Young/
Rex Features; Jun Sato/ WireImage/ Getty Images;
Juan Naharro Gimenez/ WireImage/ Getty Images;
David Rowland/ AAP/ Press Association Images;
Neil Mockford/ FilmMagic/ Getty Images; Dennis
Van Tine/ ABACA USA/ Empics Entertainment/
Press Association Images; IBL/ Rex Features;
Beretta/ Sims/ Rex Features; Kevin Mazur/
WireImage/ Getty Images; Dave J. Hogan/ Getty
Images; Matt Crossick/ Empics Entertainment/
Press Association Images; Stuart Wilson/ Getty
Images; Action Press/ Rex Features; Simon James/
FilmMagic/ Getty Images; Stuart Wilson/ Getty
Images; Paul Smith/ Featureflash/ Shutterstock; Jon
Furniss/ Invision/ Press Association Images; Dave
M. Benett/ Getty Images; Mr Pics/ Shutterstock;
Jo Hale/ Redferns via Getty Images; Splash News/
Corbis; Dave M. Benett/ Getty Images; PA Wire/
PA Archive/ Press Association Images; Mike
Marsland/ WireImage/ Getty Images; Kevin Mazur/
WireImage/ Getty Images; FOX/ Getty Images;
Kevin Kane/ Getty Images; Startraks Photo/ Rex
Features; Kevin Mazur/ WireImage/ Getty Images;
Tom Meinelt/ Splash News/ Corbis; Kevin Mazur/
Getty Images; Mark Cuthbert/ UK Press via Getty
Images; Tim Whitby/ WireImage/ Getty Images;
Sara Jaye/ Rex Features; Kenzo Tribouillard/ AFP/
Getty Images; Sara Jaye/ Rex Features; Comic
Relief/ Splash News/ Corbis; Dave M. Benett/ Getty
Images; Brian Rasic/ Rex Features; Richard Young/
Rex Features; Dave J. Hogan/ Getty Images;
Richard Young/ Rex Features.